A CLOSER WALK

DEVOTIONS BY
STEVE TROXEL

VOLUME 2

A CLOSER WALK
Volume 2

Published by

God's Daily Word Ministries
http://www.gdwm.org

ISBN 0-9708531-5-7
Copyright © 2004
by
God's Daily Word Ministries.

Written by Steve Troxel

Cover Design by Al Mendenhall
Creative Vision Studio, San Antonio, Texas

Printed in Canada

CONTENTS

CONTENTS

PREFACE

In August of 1996, as my wife and I were on the way to the hospital for the birth of our daughter, I sent a short email to a few friends and family. Unaware at the time, this was the beginning of God's Daily Word Ministries. The updates on my daughter's birth changed to short words of encouragement and scripture verses, and later grew to full devotionals.

Over the last several years, God has led thousands of people from all over the world to be a part of this growing ministry. This has been a wonderful journey of ever increasing faith and trust.

God has taught me that His main message is a continuous call to draw nearer and to love and trust Him more. This is His message when He first calls us to believe in Jesus for the forgiveness of sin and be restored to a relationship which has been broken for so long. It's also His message when we have journeyed with Him for a long while but are continuously subject to the pulls of the world.

This book is the second volume of what is intended to be a six volume set. The devotional messages in each of these books are written to give some instruction from God's Word as well as application and encouragement to draw nearer to God through trust, love and worship. These messages are for those who are seeking as well as those who have trusted Jesus for many years. I firmly believe that, no matter where we are in our relationship with God, we ALL are being called to A Closer Walk!

Steve Troxel

THE BABY GREW

It's a new year and time to start back into our routines – Christmas is over and it's time to get back to work and recover from the holidays. We've enjoyed celebrating the birth of Jesus and seeing Him peacefully sleeping in a manger, but now it's time to pack Him away until next year. What?? Steve, I can't believe you said that!

Unfortunately, many around the world give Jesus center stage for a short season around Christmas and then continue with their "normal" life while keeping Christ tucked conveniently out of sight. But let's take a close look at what just happened.

The promised baby was born among the animals in the town of Bethlehem; "She wrapped Him in cloths and placed Him in a manger, because there was no room for them in the inn" (Luke 2:7). The wonderful image of baby Jesus in a manger has, for many, become the complete picture of Christmas. The baby is easy to celebrate: He's cute; He's gentle; and He asks nothing of us. While lying in a manger, Jesus requires no decision or commitment. It's even easy to love baby Jesus without ever facing the truth that He loved us first, and loves us now more than we can possibly comprehend.

But as we leave this Christmas season and prayerfully grow in our relationship with God, we MUST not leave the baby in the manger or pack Him away. The baby was a precious gift from our Heavenly Father, but the purpose of this gift was for the baby to grow...and then to die...and then to live again! Jesus walked this earth for 33 years and then: "Jesus called out with a loud voice, 'Father, into Your hands I commit My spirit.' When He had said this, He breathed His last" (Luke 23:46). Jesus lived to do the will of the Father, and He died on a cross to set us free - this is why the baby was born!

John 3:14-16

> *"The Son of Man must be lifted up, that everyone who believes in Him may have eternal life. For God so loved the world that He gave His one and only Son, that whoever believes in Him shall not perish but have eternal life."*

Remembering the birth of Jesus causes us to reflect on God's love and gives us reason to say, "Thank You!" But remembering His life and death requires a decision; "Whoever believes in the Son has eternal life, but whoever rejects the Son will not see life, for God's wrath remains on him" (John 3:36).

Jesus was (and is) the One who provides the way to eternal life, but only for those who truly believe in His sacrifice for the forgiveness of sin. As another Christmas season passes, let's continue to reflect on the complete purpose of His birth. Let's keep Him at our side for every step of this new year and always remember...the baby grew!

PREPARING GOD'S PEOPLE TO SERVE

Jesus' ministry on earth lasted only three short years, but His message continues to be preached today and has spread to nearly every country and language of the world. When Jesus began His ministry, He knew His time would quickly pass. Yet rather than trying to preach to the greatest number of people, Jesus focused the majority of His effort on a small group of twelve men.

Jesus taught His disciples about the Kingdom of God and how they must learn to truly love; "By this all men will know that you are My disciples, if you love one another" (John 13:35). He taught them about the forgiveness of sin through His sacrificial death, and about their true source of strength: "Remain in Me, and I will remain in you...apart from Me you can do nothing" (John 15:4,5).

Jesus intensely taught His twelve closest followers with one overriding purpose - He taught so they would be prepared to serve in the Kingdom of God: "Go and make disciples of all nations, baptizing them...and teaching them to obey everything I have commanded you" (Matthew 28:19-20). Jesus provided a model for effective ministry which we ought to follow today.

Ephesians 4:11-12

"It was He who gave some to be apostles, some to be prophets, some to be evangelists, and some to be pastors and teachers, to prepare God's people for works of service, so that the body of Christ may be built up."

Each of us are called to be a disciple - a close and intimate follower of Jesus Christ. We are given different gifts and different ministry opportunities; but the focus of a disciple is always to serve as we build up the body of Christ and love Him with all our heart. We help others become His disciple as we teach them to follow Jesus and provide the necessary tools which prepare them to serve.

We have been blessed in so many ways. By His grace we have been granted the forgiveness of all sin and given a place to worship Him for all eternity. As we better grasp this wonderful truth, we will be filled with an unshakable contentment and peace while we walk in the presence of God. But this blessing must never be selfishly held - it must be shared; "Freely you have received, freely give" (Matthew 10:8).

I pray that every day brings us closer in our relationship with God through the forgiveness and love of His Son Jesus. I pray we minister in our church, our work, our family, and among the friends God places in our path with love and uncompromising truth. And I pray that each of us look for ways to build up the body of Christ by preparing God's people to serve.

HIS BURDEN IS LIGHT

In the message "Preparing God's People to Serve" we saw how Jesus set the example for ministry by equipping others to serve in His Kingdom. We also saw that each of us have been called to minister as we love Him and build up the body of Christ. Our specific roles in ministry may differ, but we have all been called and asked be a part of His plan. We are given the charge to tell others of the way to the Father through faith in Jesus. Paul calls this the ministry of reconciliation; "We are therefore Christ's ambassadors, as though God were making His appeal through us" (2 Corinthians 5:20).

But ministry (in any form) can be difficult. There is more work to be done in the field than we can possibly accomplish - our "job" is never complete. This has the potential for great stress (and what we call "burnout") if we don't maintain a sense of our true purpose and a sense of Who is really in charge.

Matthew 11:28-30

"Come to Me, all you who are weary and burdened, and I will give you rest. Take My yoke upon you and learn from Me, for I am gentle and humble in heart, and you will find rest for your souls. For My yoke is easy and My burden is light."

A yoke is a dual harness used to attach to oxen and plow the fields. Jesus said to take up His yoke and join Him in working the field. He's already pulling the load and wants us to attach ourselves to the other harness. As we do, we will discover a well-defined row in bad need of plowing - we will also find a load which is easy to bear.

But plowing can become tedious so we often try to increase the pace. We look for ways to accomplish more and begin to see the many weeds scattered in other rows and other fields. In an attempt to pull as many weeds as possible we begin to wander from our row and our load becomes increasingly heavy. We soon find we have unhitched from His yoke and are trying to pull the plow with our own strength.

More is not always better and faster is not always the desired result. It's interesting that Jesus said our main task as we take up His yoke is to "learn from Him." It's as if walking by His side is really enough. The field will still get plowed, but in the process we will be blessed with a closer and deeper relationship with Him.

If our burden has become heavy - if we're feeling weary and ready to quit - let's determine if we are properly "hitched" to His yoke and aligned to His row. A heavy burden requires some adjustments - maybe an adjustment in attitude, maybe an adjustment in priority. Let's ask our Heavenly Father for guidance and where to find rest for our soul. Let's take up His yoke and remember: His burden is light!

SHINY STONES

There are many types of monkey which can be captured with nothing more than a hollow wooden ball and a few shiny stones. The wooden ball contains a hole just large enough for the open hand of the monkey to pass through. The shiny stones are placed inside the ball and the ball is then tied to a tree.

The curious monkey reaches into the hollow ball and grasps the stones but then finds his hand will no longer pass through the hole while he clings to his prize. The monkey fights to free his hand but will not drop the stones and is therefore easily captured.

This is a fun story - but I don't really think it's true. Monkeys are actually much smarter than this illustration makes them appear. But I wonder how many of us are being trapped by similar tactics.

Jesus had chosen His twelve disciples and was giving them instructions as He sent them out to minister. He told them where to go and some of the hardships to expect. He also told them one of the great secrets of a successful journey.

Matthew 10:39

"Whoever finds his life will lose it, and whoever loses his life for My sake will find it."

Another translation of this same verse reads: "If you cling to your life, you will lose it; but if you give it up for Me, you will find it." This is a truth the world doesn't want us to hear: the only way to find the freedom of true life is to let go and give Him our complete trust.

We are saved only by grace through faith in Jesus Christ (Ephesians 2:8) - but a saving faith must be faith in the complete Jesus, all He is and all He represents! He came as our Savior: the Lamb who was sacrificed for the forgiveness of our sin. But He also came as the Son of God, our Sovereign Lord. A saving faith cannot pick and choose what portion of Jesus to accept; we either let go and give Him our complete trust or we show we have rejected Him as we cling to self-control.

The world is packed full of "trappings" which lure us and keep us from surrendering to Jesus as Lord. We're continually enticed to follow "The Road to Happiness" with promises of pleasure and power; but if we look close we'll see nothing but a handful of worthless stones which keep us from true freedom.

We can no longer cling to the empty values of the world; we must let go and present ourselves to God as a living sacrifice (Romans 12:1). If we want to find the freedom of true life, we must have a faith which allows us to lose our life to the will of our Lord - we must be willing to let go of our shiny stones.

TAKE UP OUR CROSS

In the message "Shiny Stones" we saw how we are often trapped by the seductive temptations of the world and kept from a truly free life - a life found only through complete surrender to Jesus; "Whoever finds his life will lose it, and whoever loses his life for My sake will find it" (Matthew 10:39). This may seem a little radical - maybe only something for those "really serious" Christians - but God's Word clearly sets this as the standard for all His children.

Matthew 10:38

"Anyone who does not take his cross and follow Me is not worthy of Me."

Luke records similar words as Jesus spoke to a large crowd: "and anyone who does not carry his cross and follow Me cannot be My disciple" (Luke 14:27). Jesus also said that anyone who would come after Him must "take up his cross daily and follow" (Luke 9:23).

But what does it mean to take up our cross? I've heard people refer to a hardship or difficult situation as "my cross to bear," but God's Word contains no such reference. The cross has only one Biblical association: Death! The only time anyone would carry their cross was when they were about to die.

Yes, we are called to die. But the call is not to a physical death - this death will eventually come to all and there's never a need to hasten its arrival. The call of Jesus is to a death of "self," the old sinful nature with its evil desires, dreams, and ambitions: "I have been crucified with Christ and I no longer live, but Christ lives in me. The life I live in this body, I live by faith in the Son of God" (Galatians 2:20).

This is a death which leads to true contentment and peace. But this death is not a one time event, nor is it easy. We are called to die daily! Don't be surprised when every day seems to bring life to our old nature - when we seem to talk, act, and think contrary to the way of Christ. When this occurs, simply praise God for the conviction of His Spirit, take up the cross, and continue to follow down His path.

As we "die" and completely surrender control to God, temptations of the world lose their pull and anxieties lose their source of concern. As we no longer live, we no longer focus on the cravings of our flesh nor about what tomorrow may or may not bring. As Christ lives in us, the enemy loses their ability to effectively attack - they are no longer attacking us but Christ!

Our call is to become a follower of Jesus Christ and be transformed into His image, but to follow we must die. Let's become His worthy disciple as we love Him and trust Him with all our heart. Let's set aside all that is not directed by God and take up our cross.

LIGHT AND MOMENTARY

There is no more dramatic example of a Christ-changed life than the Apostle Paul. While on his way to Damascus to capture Christians and put them in jail, Jesus blinded Paul and asked: "Why do you persecute Me?" (Acts 9:4). When Paul asked who was speaking, Jesus replied: "I am Jesus, whom you are persecuting. Now get up and go into the city, and you will be told what you must do" (Acts 9:5-6).

Jesus identified Paul as "My chosen instrument to carry My name before the Gentiles and their kings and before the people of Israel" (Acts 9:15). This special selection did not make Paul perfect, but he was gifted with a close relationship with Jesus as well as special insight into the true gospel message.

Paul suffered many hardships and trials during his years of ministry. His life was continually threatened; he was beaten many times, placed in prison for extended periods, and faced the frustration of ministering to people who failed to truly appreciate his message. And yet, Paul weighed his trials on the scale of eternity.

2 Corinthians 4:16-17

"Therefore we do not lose heart. Though outwardly we are wasting away, yet

inwardly we are being renewed day by day. For our light and momentary troubles are achieving for us an eternal glory that far outweighs them all."

Paul had learned "the secret of being content in any and every situation" (Philippians 4:12). This secret involved knowing who he was in Christ and viewing his life from the perspective of eternity. This secret gave him a new understanding of his trials.

Our life must no longer be viewed with a beginning and an end, but truly as being eternal. Though our days on earth may sometimes be difficult, our days are very few. A hundred years is not even a visible speck on the canvas of eternity. And the weight of our burdens vanish to nothing when compared to the glory of Heaven. This is the lasting power of an eternal perspective.

God's peace and contentment requires us to expand our view to include an eternity we cannot see and a glory we may not understand. "I have told you these things, so that in Me you may have peace" (John 16:33). His peace is available today; it's available in our relationships, our work, our finances, our health, and our ministry.

Let's allow the world to see our confidence in His promised eternal glory by the peace which fills our life. Let's live by the faith of an eternal perspective and be renewed as we rightly consider ALL our trials to be light and momentary.

TIMES OF WAITING

As Paul was returning to Jerusalem at the end of his third missionary journey, he already had a sense of where his next journey would lead; "after I have been there, I must visit Rome" (Acts 19:21). But he also knew he was about to face many difficulties; "in every city the Holy Spirit warns me that prison and hardships are facing me" (Acts 20:23). Paul was arrested less than ten days after arriving in Jerusalem. He probably didn't realize it at the time, but his journey to Rome had just begun.

Paul's journey to Rome would last about two and a half years and include many legal and physical trials - and many opportunities to demonstrate his faith in Jesus Christ. Surprisingly, it also included two long years where Paul had nothing to do but sit in prison and wait for an occasional visit with the Governor before being transferred to the courts of Rome.

Acts 24:25

"As Paul discoursed on righteousness, self-control and the judgment to come, Felix was afraid and said, 'That's enough for now! You may leave. When I find it convenient, I will send for you.'"

This must have been a difficult time for someone accustomed to being so actively involved in ministry. Paul was treated well in this prison, but after receiving specific instructions to minister in Rome, two years must have felt like a painfully long time.

We're never told of God's reason for this waiting period. Many times, waiting is necessary to allow other events to occur and other people to be properly positioned; and many times, waiting is necessary because we need to better learn some of God's truths, or simply need a good rest.

Paul was about to face his most challenging journey and possibly his most significant ministry opportunity; "Take courage! As you have testified about Me in Jerusalem, so you must also testify in Rome" (Acts 23:11). On his journey, Paul faced a severe storm, shipwreck, snakebite, and many threats on his life; but Paul was also given the opportunity to minister to the leaders of the Roman Empire.

Much of our own journey involves patience and learning how to trust and wait on God. Almost nothing seems to occur as fast as we would like: difficult situations take longer to resolve, people take longer to mature, and ministries take longer to grow. But our present circumstances always serve a purpose!

If we've earnestly sought God and not received specific direction, it's possible we're simply being told to wait - wait and be refreshed; wait and spend time abiding in His presence; wait...and prepare. Let's continue to rejoice and learn to trust Him even more during our times of waiting.

STAND ON SOLID GROUND

In the last two messages, we've been encouraged that as we begin to view our life more
from God's perspective - an eternal perspective - our heavy burdens can seem "Light and
Momentary" and we can find purpose even in
our "Times of Waiting." But this view cannot
be truly obtained apart from belief in Jesus
Christ. It's a life changing benefit found only
through an understanding of the gospel.

The gospel message is one of hope which
says, God loves us and has an ETERNAL plan
for our life through faith in His Son Jesus.
Without the hope of the gospel, we would
continue to live a life of emptiness and an
eternity separated from God. Even if we were
to stumble onto temporary fulfillment, without
the gospel our life would end without hope.

But as we place our trust in Jesus for the forgiveness of our sin, He lifts us up, gives our
life new meaning, and transforms us into a new
creation through the power of His Spirit.

Psalm 40:1-2

> *"I waited patiently for the Lord; He
> turned to me and heard my cry. He lifted
> me out of the slimy pit, out of the mud and
> mire; He set my feet on a rock and gave
> me a firm place to stand."*

These words were written by King David over one thousand years before the death and resurrection of Jesus. And yet, they provide an excellent illustration of the hope found in the message of Salvation.

In our sinful nature, we all "have gone astray, each of us has turned to his own way" (Isaiah 53:6). Our nature is to follow our own sinful desires and walk down paths which cause us to "fall short of the glory of God" (Romans 3:23). Each of us have been firmly embedded in the mire of sin and none of us can climb out of the slimy pit with our own strength - we cannot construct an eternal hope!

But praise God that before the creation of the world He loved us and had a plan to bring us back to Himself - a plan to rescue us: "While we were still sinners, Christ died for us" (Romans 5:8). The death and resurrection of Jesus allows us victory over sin and creates a way out of the mud: "If you confess with your mouth, 'Jesus is Lord,' and believe in your heart that God raised Him from the dead, you will be saved" (Romans 10:9).

If we truly desire to be clean and live with hope and a new view of this life, we must call out to Jesus and believe He is who He claimed to be: our Savior and Lord! If we will trust Him and cry out in faith, He has promised to hear our cry and lift us up. He will pour His cleansing love upon us and fill us with purpose! He will set our feet for all eternity upon Himself and we will forever stand on solid ground.

STAND FIRM ON THE ROCK

In the message "Stand On Solid Ground" we compared Salvation through faith in Jesus to the words of praise written by David: "He lifted me out of the slimy pit, out of the mud and mire; He set my feet on a rock and gave me a firm place to stand" (Psalm 40:2). We saw how God gives us an eternal hope by lifting us up, washing us clean, and setting our feet upon a new and solid path. But what should we do now that our feet have been set?

When we are in the slimy and muddy pit we're vulnerable to attack. It's difficult to move and we easily lose our balance. We tend to live in fear, not knowing who to trust or which way to turn. But as Christ lifts us up we become "a new creation" (2 Corinthians 5:17). Life on solid ground should not be the same as life in the pit!

As the Spirit of God transforms us, He also provides everything we need to accomplish God's work and live a victorious life; "His divine power has given us everything we need for life and godliness" (2 Peter 1:3). Knowing that our Heavenly Father has created us anew and gifted us with ALL we ever need, we must now be resolved to stand firm.

1 Corinthians 15:58

"Therefore, my dear brothers, stand firm. Let nothing move you. Always give yourselves fully to the work of the Lord, because you know that your labor in the Lord is not in vain."

We must make every effort to firmly stand; and yet, we must realize that we cannot stand in our own strength. The ground is solid only because of Christ. He IS the rock upon which we have been set - the Rock of our Salvation. Whenever we feel unworthy or unable to follow - whenever we feel we can no longer stand - we have surely begun to look to our own strength rather than God: "Now it is God who makes both us and you stand firm in Christ," (2 Corinthians 1:21). He alone gives us the strength.

We have trusted Him to lift us out of the pit. Now that we are His child, we must continue to trust Him to strengthen us and be the stable Rock of our life. "For if, when we were God's enemies, we were reconciled to Him through the death of His Son, how much more, having been reconciled, shall we be saved through His life!" (Romans 5:10).

The solid Rock is no place to tremble, no place to fear. He will remain solid for all eternity; and, as we stand on Him, He will accomplish through us what we are unable to do in our own strength. He is our new life, our strength, our identity, and all our self-worth. Let's honor our Heavenly Father as we continue to stand. Let's bring Him glory as we resolve to stand firm on the Rock!

LIFT HIM UP

In the message "Stand Firm On The Rock" we saw how Christ is the solid Rock upon which we have been set. He alone is our stable source of direction and strength. We will need to visit this truth again and again as we continue to answer the call to follow.

When Jesus called Peter and Andrew to "Come, follow Me" (Matthew 4:19), He was calling them to become His disciples (the word disciple means follower). But Jesus places strong conditions on a disciple; "Anyone who does not carry his cross and follow Me cannot be My disciple" (Luke 14:27).

The call to be a disciple is not simply a call to live a good moral life; it's a call to crucify (put to death) everything of our self that hinders our relationship with God. We must hold loosely to everything but God; "Any of you who does not give up everything he has cannot be My disciple" (Luke 14:33).

The life of a disciple must clearly demonstrate a commitment to Christ by producing fruit for His Kingdom; "This is to My Father's glory, that you bear much fruit, showing yourself to be My disciple" (John 15:8). A disciple must flow with pure love; "By this all men will know that you are My disciples, if you love one another" (John 13:35). And a disciple must maintain a commitment to all Jesus taught; "If you hold to My teachings, you are really My disciples" (John 8:31).

Discipleship appears to be a VERY difficult call! It's difficult to be His disciple and even more difficult to "make disciples of all nations" (Matthew 28:19). In fact, if we focus only on these "requirements," our task is impossible. We are called to glorify God by drawing very near to Jesus and loving Him with all our heart. But in our own strength, we have no ability to draw near - no ability to be His disciple.

John 12:32

"But I, when I am lifted up from the earth, will draw all men to Myself."

When Jesus was "lifted up" on the cross and died for our sin, He provided the way back to the Father - the way to become His disciple. He drew us to Himself so we could be forgiven and stand in the presence of God. Likewise, the only way to draw near and follow today is to lift Him up to His rightful throne over our life and give Him our pure praise and absolute worship.

If we fail to lift up Christ, our efforts to carry our cross become nothing more than a list of restrictive rules; we will have no ability to produce Kingdom fruit, and our love for others will be selfish and artificial. Let's "make disciples" by first being His devoted disciple. And let's be His disciple by ensuring that in ALL we do, we love Him and continually lift Him up.

A FREE AND SECURE SERVANT

The night before Jesus was crucified He was celebrating the Passover meal with His disciples. We traditionally call this the Last Supper. Jesus knew this would be the last time He would eat with His disciples; He knew in just one more day He would be hung on a cross to die.

Knowing He only had a few short hours remaining with this select group, Jesus used His time to leave a lasting impression of what it meant to truly follow Him.

John 13:3-5

> *"Jesus knew that the Father had put all things under His power, and that He had come from God and was returning to God; so He got up from the meal, took off His outer clothing, and wrapped a towel around His waist. After that, He poured water into a basin and began to wash His disciples' feet, drying them with the towel that was wrapped around Him."*

Without using words, Jesus gave perhaps His greatest sermon. Jesus was absolutely secure in who He was and where He was going: "He had come from God and was returning to God." But He was not proud or arrogant in His security - He didn't use His position as a club to force others to submit or demand they fill His needs - instead, His secure position allowed Him to be completely humble and serve His disciples by washing their feet.

Our Heavenly Father desires for us to have this same level of security in Him. He wants us to KNOW we are His children and where we will spend eternity. Jesus came to set us free, and we are to walk in this secure freedom. But rather than using our freedom to arrogantly strut according to our own desires, a secure freedom should give us the necessary confidence to humbly serve without being offended; "do not use your freedom to indulge the sinful nature; rather, serve one another in love" (Galatians 5:13).

Being a follower of Jesus Christ means, first and foremost, that we love the Lord with ALL our heart, soul, mind and strength (Mark 12:30). But next, it means we are to love, serve, and "submit to one another out of reverence for Christ" (Ephesians 5:21). Knowing where we will spend eternity, and keeping our eyes set on this eternal perspective, allows us to focus more on the needs and concerns of others (Philippians 2:3-4) and to "use whatever gifts {we have} received to serve others" (1 Peter 4:10). My earthly needs become few when I have a clear picture of my eternal home.

Let's learn to live as Jesus lived: in fellowship with our Heavenly Father; with absolute assurance of who we are in Christ; with confidence of our eternal destiny; and with the complete abandoned humility of a free and secure servant.

GIVE FROM THE HEART

In the book of Malachi, God called the people back to the law He established 800 years earlier with Moses. God spoke of the necessity of a pure sacrifice (Malachi 1:7-8), and the need for the priests to speak a message of truth (Malachi 2:7-8). He also addressed the issue of giving back a portion of our resources - a portion referred to as the tithe.

Malachi 3:8, 10

> *"Will a man rob God? Yet you rob Me. But you ask, 'How do we rob You?' In tithes and offerings. Bring the whole tithe into the storehouse, that there may be food in My house."*

The principle of an offering began with Cain and Able (Genesis 4:3-4). Abraham then demonstrated the concept of the tithe when he gave Melchizedek "a tenth of everything" (Genesis 14:20). But systematic tithing was not established until God gave the law to Moses, (Leviticus 27:30-33).

In the time of Malachi, God not only called for a return to the discipline of tithing, He also directly linked tithing to blessings and gave the ultimate challenge: "Test Me in this and see if I will not throw open the floodgates of Heaven" (Malachi 3:10). God certainly never "owes" us because of anything we do; but His Word contains a consistent call to obedience, and true obedience always results in true blessing.

When Jesus died on the cross, He fulfilled the law for all who believe. And though the legalistic letter of the law has passed away, the intent of the law (which is the heart of God) remains for all time; "These {laws} are a shadow of the things to come; the reality, however, is found in Christ" (Colossians 2:17).

The intent, or "reality," of all the law is that God is Lord over ALL areas of our life. The law teaches this truth and shows us how far short we fall of His standard. The purpose of the law was much more than teaching us to comply with a written code. The shadow contained in the written law says "Thou shalt not kill," but the reality in Christ says to not even have hatred in our heart, (Matthew 5:21-22). The shadow in the law also says "Thou shalt not commit adultery," but the reality in Christ says to even refrain from lust (Matthew 5:27-28).

When we debate about the "rules" of how much and where to give, we are focused on the shadow and miss the reality of Christ - He is Lord of ALL! As we focus our eyes on Christ, we will give. We will give generously, "not reluctantly or under compulsion" (2 Corinthians 9:7). We will gladly give of our time, talents, and finances to whatever need He directs. When He is truly Lord, we will not simply give according to a "formula" dictated by the law, we will live under His grace and give according to the law's intent. When He is Lord, we will cease to rob God and will joyfully give our lives as we give from the heart.

FOLLOW HIM TO NINEVEH

The subject of God's will is often one of great concern to growing Christians. Those who have accepted the forgiving grace of Jesus now have a desire to live a life which brings Him glory and honor. We have read we are to present ourselves as "living sacrifices, holy and pleasing to God" (Romans 12:1), and we're ready to do His will; but what does God want us to do, where does He want us to go?

Fortunately, much of God's will is found directly in His Word. It's God's will that we live a pure and holy life (1 Thessalonians 4:3-7), and obey His commands (John 15:10). It's God's will that we love Him with all our heart, soul, mind, and strength (Mark 12:30), that we remain in Him and bear much fruit (John 15:1-8), that we forgive others (Matthew 6:14-15), love others (1 John 4:7), and share the message of Jesus with others (Matthew 28:19-20). It's also God's will to "be joyful always; pray continuously; {and} give thanks in all circumstances" (1 Thessalonians 5:16-18).

This list is not complete, but it's a good sampling of what is referred to as God's "general" will - His will for all His children as we are "conformed to the likeness of His Son" (Romans 8:29). God's general will involves a lifetime of worship and abiding in His presence. We still must pray for guidance and strength in following His general will, but we need not desperately search - His general will has already been revealed in His Word.

God's specific will for our life comes as a very direct, clear, and persistent call. This call is perhaps best demonstrated in the life of Jonah.

Jonah 1:2

"Go to the great city of Nineveh and preach against it, because its wickedness has come up before Me."

God's specific will for Jonah was clear and with a definite purpose. Jonah then had a choice whether to obey and follow. Jonah tried to run from God's will - run from Nineveh - and spent three days inside a giant fish. After the fish vomited Jonah onto dry land, God calmly revealed His will a second time; "Go to the great city of Nineveh..." (Jonah 3:2). God's call remained exactly the same; His specific will for Jonah was unchanged. This time, "Jonah obeyed the word of the Lord" (Jonah 3:3).

There are vast portions of God's will which are already revealed in His Word. We must develop the discipline of reading and studying His Word - studying His will - and then follow what He has already commanded. For the part of God's will which is specific to our life, we must listen intently, pray diligently, and wait very patiently. But when His specific direction arrives (and we will know when God calls) we must be prepared to abandon all else and boldly follow Him to Nineveh!

MINISTERING TO NINEVEH

In the message "Follow Him to Nineveh" we discussed the will of God in terms of His "general" and "specific" will. We saw that God's Word has already given a great deal of direction which applies to every Child of God. Our Heavenly Father desires each of His Children to be "conformed to the likeness of His Son" (Romans 8:29). And the process of being conformed is primarily one of obedient worship in ALL areas of our life. But then comes Nineveh!

The story of Jonah and the giant fish is one of the best known in the Bible and provides a wonderful example of how we need to follow when God calls. When God has a specific call for our life He will persistently give us clear direction and use all His infinite resources to make sure we understand. But as we read through the entire Word of God we must conclude that this type of specific call is relatively rare. For most, God's will never moves beyond a general call to walk in His love.

Yes, Jonah teaches us to follow when God's call is specific. But there's an even more important principle regarding God's general will which applies to all of us nearly every day of our life. This principle is discovered by examining why Jonah ran from God: "'Go to the great city of Nineveh and preach against it, because it's wickedness has come up before Me.' But Jonah ran away from the Lord and headed for Tarshish" (Jonah 1:2-3).

Jonah didn't run from God simply because Nineveh was located in a distant and foreign land. Jonah ran because he disliked (even hated) the people who lived in this leading city of the growing empire of Assyria. The people of Nineveh had a reputation for cruelty in war, idolatry, and a general disrespect for God. Jonah had grown up with a hatred of Nineveh and couldn't bear being sent there to preach. He couldn't bear the thought of these hated people actually repenting and being blessed by "his" God.

Jonah 4:2

"O Lord, is this not what I said when I was still at home? That is why I was so quick to flee to Tarshish. I knew that You are a gracious and compassionate God, slow to anger and abounding in love, a God who relents from sending calamity."

God desires all the world to turn from their wicked ways and receive His blessings. And His general call is for us to deliver this message of love. We are called to deliver this message to ALL - especially those we may naturally dislike or have been "taught" to fear and hate. This becomes a form of worship because it demonstrates our understanding of the grace we have been given through faith in Jesus - none of us can ever earn God's love! Let's take the general will of God into the mission field placed before us and worship our Father by accepting the challenge of ministering to Nineveh.

GRACE-FILLED HOLINESS

We often speak of God's Word as the absolute truth by which we are to live. We encourage one another to live without compromise and not to be pulled by the temptations of the world. But these type of discussions always imply a standard for Christian living; and, as much as we hate to admit it, a standard implies rules. Oh, how these words make some uncomfortable - some even angry!

Much of the Christian teaching we receive today is focused on the free gift of God's grace; "For it is by grace you have been saved" (Ephesians 2:8), and this grace seems to be in conflict with the presence of rules. Since our sins have already been forgiven, and "there is now no condemnation for those who are in Christ Jesus" (Romans 8:1), how can we talk about rules or standards or expectations?

It is absolutely clear in the Word of God that we are saved by grace and can do nothing to earn or improve upon our Salvation - we live and breathe under God's grace. However, it's also perfectly clear in His Word that there exists a standard of holiness for which we must strive. Sin is defined against a standard and the precious gift of God's grace never gives permission for sin!

Romans 6:1-2

"What shall we say, then? Shall we go on sinning so that grace may abound? By no means!"

As children of God, we now have complete freedom; "the law of the Spirit of life set me free from the law of sin and death" (Romans 8:2). But the freedom we have been given is the freedom to claim victory over sin and live a pure and holy life; "But just as He who called you is holy, so be holy in all you do" (1 Peter 1:15). We will never attain perfect holiness, never live in perfect compliance with God's standard. And though we who belong to Jesus are no longer under condemnation, we are called to live free of sin.

So why do we strive? First, holiness is honoring to God because God hates sin. Sin kills those our Father loves - those He loves so much that He sent Jesus to die as a sacrifice for the penalty of sin. God hates sin and we ought to hate what God hates. And next, as we strive for holiness (while remembering that our striving plays no part in our Salvation) we will see even more clearly how far we fall from God's required perfection. As we strive, our sin will become even more apparent and we will see with ever increasing thankfulness how much grace and forgiveness we have been given through faith in Jesus.

Salvation is ALL grace!! We live under His grace and have been set free from the law of sin and death; so now, let's truly learn of His grace by seeking to follow in His steps and striving for a thankful heart through a life of grace-filled holiness.

THE GREAT CLOUD OF WITNESSES

I ran my first marathon (January 2004) in Phoenix Arizona. I'll spare you some of the painful details of running out of energy at the twenty mile point and being passed in the last mile by a 65 year old woman (I'll run better next time!). I learned many lessons that day, but the thing that struck me the most was how the cheering crowd helped me to run faster and farther than I thought possible. The 26 mile course was lined with thousands upon thousands of people. No one except my dear family knew my name, but they were ALL shouting words of encouragement.

Our journey with the Lord is like a marathon in many ways. We must maintain a disciplined training program to ensure we are prepared. The race itself can be long and hard - there will be times we run out of energy and want to quit - but crossing the finish line will be more rewarding than anything we can imagine! And along the way, we will certainly learn to appreciate the encouragement we receive from the cheering crowd.

Hebrews 12:1

> *"Therefore, since we are surrounded by such a great cloud of witnesses, let us throw off everything that hinders and the sin that so easily entangles, and let us run*

with perseverance the race marked out for us."

This verse follows what we often refer to as The Great Hall of Faith. Hebrews, chapter 11, describes many people from the Old Testament who were commended for their faith: Able, Noah, Abraham, Joseph, Moses, Gideon, Samson, David, and many others.

At the end of this impressive list, we read that even though they were faithful, "none of them received what had been promised" (Hebrews 11:39). Their reward was postponed until the coming of Jesus; "God had planned something better for us so that only together with us would they be made perfect" (Hebrews 11:40). It's as if the faithful from the past are now watching us and cheering with great excitement and anticipation, knowing that one day we will be "caught up together with them" (1 Thessalonians 4:17) to receive our eternal reward.

This cloud of witnesses now also includes the New Testament believers as well as Christians throughout the last 2000 years. It also includes Brothers and Sisters who love us and pray for us today. As we run the race and sometimes grow weary - sometimes even stumble and fall - these witnesses continue to cheer us on and encourage our every step.

We can run faster and farther than we think! Yes, the race is long and sometimes difficult, but we're definitely not alone. Let's run with renewed perseverance; and when we become discouraged, let's listen for the cheers from the Great Cloud of Witnesses!

PROVING OUR FAITH

We begin our Christian life in faith; "For it is by grace you have been saved, through faith" (Ephesians 2:8). And just as we begin our life in faith, so we must also continue to walk in faith; "Just as you received Christ Jesus as Lord, continue to live in Him" (Colossians 2:6). We are to live in Christ, and continue to walk with Him, in the same manner as we received Him...in faith.

We cannot come to Christ without faith and we're unable to live a victorious Christian life without continuously walking in faith. Our faith is of great worth!

1 Peter 1:6-7

"For a little while you may have had to suffer grief in all kinds of trials. These have come so that your faith - of greater worth than gold, which perishes even though refined by fire - may be proved genuine and may result in praise, glory and honor when Jesus Christ is revealed."

One of the beautiful truths in God's Kingdom is that everything along our walk has a purpose; "In all things God works for the good of those who love Him" (Romans 8:28). Even our difficult times of hardship and trial are being directed by God "for the good." As we continue to love Him with all our heart, God will use our trials to reveal and strengthen our faith - and a true understanding of our faith is one of the greatest "goods" we can receive.

Do we really believe our faith is "of greater worth than gold"? Until we've been sustained through times of great trial and testing, it's difficult to understand the true value of faith. Our faith is shown to be real ("proved genuine") only as we trust Him when no other hope can be seen. We never need to prove our faith to God - He sees deep within our heart and already knows the genuineness of our faith. God gave us our faith and calls us to live "in accordance with the measure of faith {He} has given" (Romans 12:3).

But our measure of faith is ALWAYS greater than what we believe we have, and can sustain us through greater trials than we believe possible. As we more clearly see the strength contained in this wonderful gift of faith, we are able to give all praise, glory and honor to God as Jesus is revealed through the testimony of our life. As we trust Him with all our heart, He will cause us to emerge from our trials much stronger and more confident, more "mature and complete, not lacking anything" (James 1:4), because we will KNOW He is by our side.

As our faith is strengthened and refined, the presence of God will cease to be an interesting theory or an empty hope; it will become real and an integral part of our life! Let's rejoice that our trials last only "for a little while" - but let's also rejoice that our trials are being used for His glory and for the purpose of proving our faith.

LIVE DAILY BY FAITH

In the message "Proving Our Faith" we saw
how our faith is revealed and strengthened as
we walk through our trials. It's not surprising
that we often discuss the importance of faith,
for "without faith it is impossible to please
God" (Hebrews 11:6). If we desire to live a life
pleasing to God, we must increase our faith and
learn what it means to live by faith.

2 Corinthians 5:7

"We live by faith and not by sight."

The first step of faith is when we recognize
our sinful condition, repent of our sin, and
believe Jesus died so our sin can be forgiven.
This belief in Jesus is not a result of what we
see, but a result of faith - and without this
first step of faith it is definitely not possible to
please God.

As we continue our walk with Christ, He
becomes more and more real. Each time our
faith is strengthened, our eyes are opened a little
wider and we are allowed to see a little clearer.
The challenges of yesterday which required
great faith have become easier to bear...for now
we can see!

But the increase of Spiritual sight is not the
same as an increase of faith. As our Spiritual
sight grows, our need for faith in order to walk

the same path is actually reduced; "Now faith is being sure of what we hope for and certain of what we do not see" (Hebrews 11:1). True faith always involves a confidence of the unknown, an assurance of what is unseen.

Our Heavenly Father desires to lead us in a life of faith. He continues to draw us into the unknown, for it is only in the unknown that we truly learn to "trust in the Lord with all your heart and lean not on your own understanding" (Proverbs 3:5). And as the unknown becomes known, He will surely call us to take the next step and trust Him more.

Where is God calling us today? For some it's to take the awesome step required for Salvation through faith in Jesus; "Today if you hear His voice, do not harden your hearts" (Hebrews 4:7). For some it's a step of trust for a burden which right now seems completely unbearable; and for some, it's a step into a level of service which appears impossible to achieve. Each of these require a step into the unknown, into a place we cannot see; but each is part of the great adventure of faith!

Though the unknown is sometimes uncomfortable and maybe even a little scary, being guided by God into what we cannot see is the essence of a life of faith - a life which pleases God. Until the day He calls us Home, we must continue to listen, step, and grow - we must continue to live daily by faith.

CREATE LASTING MEMORIALS

After the people of Israel wandered in the desert for 40 years, God led them across the Jordan river into the promised land of Canaan. This was not an ordinary river crossing. God stopped the Jordan from flowing and allowed the priests to stand in the middle of the river bed with the ark of the covenant as the Israelites walked passed. This spectacular event was an obvious miracle that God wanted His people to remember and pass down to future generations.

Joshua 4:5-7

> *"Each of you is to take up a stone on his shoulder, according to the number of the tribes of the Israelites, to serve as a sign among you. In the future, when your children ask you, 'What do these stones mean?' tell them that the flow of the Jordan was cut off before the ark of the covenant of the Lord. When it crossed the Jordan, the waters of the Jordan were cut off. These stones are to be a memorial to the people of Israel forever.'"*

Memorials are anything that help us remember a specific time when God revealed Himself and said: "I am here!" We must never forget the miracles in our life, nor the times God gave us clear direction or rescued us from darkness.

When David went to fight Goliath, he did so without fear because he knew: "The Lord who delivered me from the paw of the lion and the paw of the bear will deliver me from the hand of this Philistine" (1 Samuel 17:37). David had seen God's power and felt His presence during previous battles. It's easy to imagine David with a lion's tooth or a bear's claw around his neck as a reminder that God was very near.

The presence of God is a wonderful place to be - it's where our Heavenly Father desires for us to live each day of our life! But His presence can often be illusive and fragile; when we find it, it seems to quickly fade away. Most of us have so much input from the world that we become easily distracted from God. We must not allow this to happen!!

We must become more aware of God as He works in our life and in the world around us. As we see and hear Him, we must find ways to create memories for ourselves and those we love; "I will remember the deeds of the Lord; yes, I will remember your miracles of long ago" (Psalm 77:11). Memorials help and encourage us to remember.

Let's never forget He is by our side and desires for us to draw, and remain, near. Let's be a living example of a life devoted (each and every moment) to God. Let's regain the heart of worship and share the stories of God's love. Let's remember...and look for ways to create lasting memorials.

WHOM WE WILL SERVE

Joshua led the people of Israel into the promised land of Canaan and helped them fight many battles. Toward the end of his life, Joshua gathered the leaders of Israel for some final encouragement: "You yourselves have seen everything the Lord your God has done to all these nations for your sake; it was the Lord your God who fought for you" (Joshua 23:3).

Joshua wanted the leaders to know that God would continue to fight for them; but he also wanted them to know that God expected obedience to His Word: "If you violate the covenant of the Lord your God, and go and serve other gods and bow down to them, the Lord's anger will burn against you" (Joshua 23:16). Joshua then gathered all the people and told them the time had come to make a choice.

Joshua 24:15

"But if serving the Lord seems undesirable to you, then choose for yourselves this day whom you will serve, whether the gods your forefathers served beyond the river, or the gods of the Amorites, in whose land you are living. But as for me and my household, we will serve the Lord."

The Israelites had seen God's mighty hand as they fought their enemies in Canaan and had heard many stories of God's protection as He led them out of Egypt - the time had now come to make a decision. Either they would commit to serve the Lord with ALL their heart, or they would serve the man made gods of the world.

We face the same decision today. We either decide to follow and serve Jesus, or we have decided to serve the priorities and "gods" of this world. "Whoever believes in Him is not condemned, but whoever does not believe stands condemned already because he has not believed in the name of God's one and only Son" (John 3:18). There is no middle ground, a choice must be made! And failure to choose is itself a choice.

Everyone must make their own decision about Jesus, but each of us have a wonderful opportunity to influence others - especially those in our family. Notice that Joshua boldly spoke for his entire home: "WE will serve the Lord!" We can't force others to drink (and we can't quench their thirst by drinking for them), but we can definitely lead them to the water.

We can no longer float through life waiting to see where the pulls of this world will lead; we must live with intention and purpose, and decide once and for all to serve God with unrestricted devotion. Today, we stand at a crossroad and must choose. Today, we must choose whom we will serve.

THE COURTS OF GOD

The moment we enter through the Gate of Jesus Christ, by believing in Him for the forgiveness of our sins, we dramatically altered our eternity; "I am the gate; whoever enters through Me will be saved" (John 10:9). We were once blind and destined for eternal separation from God, but now we "see" and will spend eternity as His child in Heaven. After passing through the Gate, God begins to conform us "to the likeness of His Son" (Romans 8:29), until our sole desire is to bring Him glory, and praise His name forever.

At times, this process can be painful. It can hurt to strip away layers of pride and crawl from under the dominion of our old sinful nature - it can hurt to be conformed to the likeness of Jesus. But as we persevere and catch a glimpse of His glory, we will never again desire to be away from His presence.

Psalm 84:10

> *"Better is one day in Your courts than a thousand elsewhere; I would rather be a doorkeeper in the house of my God than dwell in the tents of the wicked."*

A single day in the presence of God is better than a thousand days anywhere else - better than ANYTHING this world can offer. If we do not believe this truth, we have not yet been in His presence - we have not yet tasted the sweet fruit of His Spirit. And if we believe and have experienced the peaceful joy of His courts but are now consumed and burdened by the trials of this world, then perhaps we've simply forgotten how sweet and fulfilling His presence can be.

Let me paraphrase the second part of the above verse: "I would rather be the lowest and most insignificant servant in the house of God, so I could be near Him, than to live as a ruler in the greatest of mansions but apart from His presence." This passion to be in the presence of God is also recorded earlier: "My soul yearns, even faints, for the courts of the Lord; my heart and my flesh cry out for the living God" (Psalm 84:2).

Our Heavenly Father longs for us to have this same passion in our life; "Enter His gates with thanksgiving and His courts with praise" (Psalm 100:4). And if this passion has faded due to distractions and entanglements, then He's calling us to return. The courts of God's holy temple now reside within every believer; "Don't you know that you yourselves are God's temple and that His Spirit lives in you" (1 Corinthians 3:16). His presence is available to us right now! No matter how distant we feel, He's closer than we think.

Let's fill His temple with praise! Let's return to a life focused on passionate worship. Let's determine to spend every moment of every day rejoicing in the courts of God.

GET ALONE AND PRAY

In the message "The Courts of God" we saw how the presence of God is to be cherished above all else. We considered that not even a thousand days in an earthly paradise can compare to a single day in the presence of God. And yet, though we may understand the value of His presence, we seldom make the decisions or exercise the discipline required to enter.

Luke 5:15-16

"The news about Him spread all the more, so the crowds of people came to hear Him and to be healed of their sicknesses. But Jesus often withdrew to lonely places and prayed."

Jesus had a relationship with the Father which can only be described as absolute perfection; "If you really knew Me, you would know My Father as well. Anyone who has seen Me has seen the Father" (John 14:7,9). We long for and desperately seek the presence of God, but Jesus Christ IS the very presence of God: "In the beginning was the Word, and the Word was with God, and the Word was God. The Word became flesh and made His dwelling among us" (John 1:1,14).

And though He had perfect union with the Father, created the entire Universe, and demonstrated complete control over the elements of nature as He "rebuked the wind and the raging waters" (Luke 8:24), Jesus still made time to be alone with the Father in prayer. Why?

Prior to the important decision of choosing His twelve apostles, Jesus "went out to a mountainside and spent the night praying" (Luke 6:12). On the night before He was crucified, Jesus was in such anguish that He prayed until "His sweat was like drops of blood falling to the ground" (Luke 22:44). Jesus, through His life and death, taught us how we ought to relate to God...and it's a lesson we must not ignore!

If Jesus, who is Perfection, demonstrated such need of prayer, how much more necessary is it for us who contain so many flaws and so easily drift away from God. We cannot wave our hand to calm the storm, we must pray for patience and strength to endure, and relentlessly ask for His help. We are to live in such constant communion with God that we "pray continually" (1 Thessalonians 5:17), even as we drive in busy traffic, manage multiple assignments, or care for noisy children.

But each of us must also set aside time, which is "often" and regular, where we can withdraw to a quiet place. Yes, the presence of God can be found in the midst of our busyness, but we all need times of quiet where we can be refreshed and receive direction - times when we can simply lift our hearts to God and say "Thank You!" Let's develop and maintain the discipline of entering the courts of His presence. Let's regularly set aside times of quiet to get alone and pray.

THE BURNING BUSH

In the last two messages we've considered the high value placed on being in the courts of God where we are able to worship in His presence. We also saw the need for quiet times of prayer in order to strengthen our relationship with God and receive His direction. No walk of submission and obedience can be complete without actually spending time with God to hear where He is leading.

Moses was born a Hebrew slave under Egyptian rule, but circumstances allowed him to be raised as a prince in Pharaoh's court (Exodus 2:1-10). As a young man, Moses began to see the injustice toward the Hebrews. At one point he took matters into his own hands and killed an Egyptian for mistreating a Hebrew slave. This action caused Moses to be misunderstood by the Hebrews and hunted by the Egyptians, so he fled across the desert to the land of Midian where he settled as a shepherd.

Going from Egyptian prince to Midianite shepherd was quite a change. As a prince, Moses received the finest education as well as the most advanced military training; but it was as a simple shepherd that Moses received the training he most needed to accomplish God's work.

Moses was a peaceful shepherd for 40 years; but then…"The angel of the Lord appeared to him in flames of fire from within a bush" (Exodus 3:2). The bush was on fire but not actually being burned. This definitely got Moses' attention so he went to take a closer look.

Exodus 3:4

"When the Lord saw that he had gone over to look, God called to him from within the bush, 'Moses! Moses!' And Moses said, 'Here I am.'"

Notice that God waited until Moses saw the bush, stopped what he was doing, and drew himself near. I wonder how long this bush had been burning before Moses noticed? During the last 40 years, how many "burning bushes" were placed in his path? "Be still, and know that I am God" (Psalm 46:10). How long had Moses needed to experience the "stillness" of tending the flock before he was ready to hear God?

God is at work all around us, and He's calling us to join Him today. The bushes are burning, but in the hurriedness of our daily lives we most often fail to notice - fail to stop and draw near. Is it any wonder we have a hard time hearing His call? I'm afraid it will be a sad day when God allows us to look back and see the life we might have lived if we would only have taken time to listen.

Let's not miss the opportunity to participate in God's wonderful plan. Let's create time to be very still and look intently for where God is working. Then, with great expectation, let's join Him and draw near to the burning bush.

STANDING ON HOLY GROUND

In the message "The Burning Bush" we saw how God spoke to Moses in a miraculous way. And, although we don't know for sure, we considered that God may have placed several burning bushes along Moses' path and called him in a variety of ways during his time as a shepherd to determine when he was ready to really listen.

When Moses approached the bush and heard God call his name, he simply replied "Here I am" (Exodus 3:4). Moses had no idea how the next few moments would change his life. Initially, he didn't even know it was God who called. But God was at work, and Moses' answer signaled his availability.

However, though Moses drew near and was available, he was not yet prepared to hear God's call.

Exodus 3:5

> *"'Do not come any closer,' God said. 'Take off your sandals, for the place where you are standing is holy ground.'"*

Sandals were in constant contact with the ground. They were continually stepping in dirt, and "other messes" left from the animals. It was unthinkable to allow something so unclean to be in contact with the holy ground of God's presence. This act of reverence was expected - even demanded - by God.

Our relationship with Jesus Christ should produce great assurance; "In Him and through faith in Him we may approach God with freedom and confidence" (Ephesians 3:12). But as we approach the throne, we must always remember He is the King and the Creator of ALL things. He has invited us into an intimate relationship, but we must never attempt to enter into God's presence with a casual or assuming attitude.

If we desire to hear from God, we must first establish time which is free of distractions - we must be able to see where He is burning and listen for His call. Then we must have an available heart which daily cries out "Here I am!" Finally, we must draw near in reverent and humble submission.

The presence of God demands holiness, it creates holiness...it IS holiness! "For it is written: 'Be holy, because I am holy'" (1 Peter 1:16). Without the presence of God, our churches and homes are nothing but walls and a roof; and our lives are nothing but empty shells of flesh. But as we love and worship Him with all our heart, His presence resides within us and we can live with purpose and direction.

Through faith in Jesus we have become His living temple. Let's take off our sandals by confessing and repenting of ALL that is unclean in our life. Let's live every day and take every step to honor Him; for we are His, and we are standing on holy ground.

IT'S ALL ABOUT HIM

In the last two messages, we've considered Moses' encounter with God as He spoke through the burning bush. Moses heard the call of God and signaled his availability, "Here I am" (Exodus 3:4). But God had an assignment for Moses that required complete trust, and preparation began by establishing the holiness of the One who was calling; "Take off your sandals, for the place where you are standing is holy ground" (Exodus 3:5).

God's chosen people had lived in Egyptian slavery for more than four hundred years. Now, God chose Moses to be His messenger and instrument of power; "I am sending you to Pharaoh to bring My people the Israelites out of Egypt" (Exodus 3:10). On one hand God's call is always a great honor - on the other, it can be very frightening.

Moses gave every possible excuse to convince God He'd made a wrong choice: "Who am I to go to Pharaoh?" (3:11), "What if they do not believe me?" (4:1), "I am slow of speech and tongue" (4:10). God was patient with Moses, but finally He had enough.

Exodus 4:11-14

"The Lord said to him, 'Who gave man his mouth? Who makes him deaf or mute?

Who gives him sight or makes him blind? Is it not I, the Lord? Now go; I will help you speak and will teach you what to say.' But Moses said, 'O Lord, please send someone else to do it.' Then the Lord's anger burned against Moses."

Moses would later be described as "more humble than anyone else on the face of the earth" (Numbers 12:2). But now, standing before God and receiving his assignment for battle, his "humility" was nothing more than a self absorbed lack of faith. Moses looked at his own abilities and didn't see how success was possible. He failed to see the Creator of the Universe who promised to walk by His side.

Our Christian walk is ALL about God working through us. Of course our abilities will seem too small, of course the enemy will seem too big! The seemingly impossible steps are all part of His plan. Our Heavenly Father desires an intimate and passionate relationship built on absolute trust. Why would He lead us in a direction that did not require our complete dependence on Him? The assignment may seem impossible, but His call is our greatest assurance of victory; "If God be for us, who can be against us" (Romans 8:31).

When God is truly Lord of our life, it's false humility to believe we cannot follow where He leads. Let's allow His glory to so completely fill our vision that we can boldly follow because we KNOW...it's all about Him.

TRUST AND MOVE ON

Moses received clear instruction as God spoke to him from the burning bush; "I am sending you to Pharaoh to bring My people the Israelites out of Egypt" (Exodus 3:10). Moses debated with God regarding his assignment and pushed God to the limit of His patience: "The Lord's anger burned against Moses" (Exodus 4:14).

But once he began to follow, Moses maintained a close relationship with God and witnessed His mighty Hand in many different ways. God worked through Moses to bring plagues against the Egyptians and to miraculously bring the Israelites out of Egypt. As Pharaoh released the Israelites and they began their journey into the desert, Moses witnessed more of God's power; "By day the Lord went ahead of them in a pillar of cloud to guide them on their way and by night in a pillar of fire to give them light" (Exodus 13:21).

But as the Israelites approached the Red Sea, "Pharaoh and his officials changed their mind" (Exodus 14:5). Every chariot in Egypt was sent to bring the Israelites back. With no escape route in sight, and the Egyptian army closing in, the people cried out to God. Moses tried to calm the people, "The Lord will fight for you: you need only to be still" (Exodus 14:14), but being still was not in God's plan.

Exodus 14:15-16

"Then the Lord said to Moses, 'Why are you crying out to Me? Tell the Israelites to move on. Raise your staff and stretch out your hand over the sea to divide the water so that the Israelites can go through the sea on dry ground.'"

God had been in close communion with Moses. He had given His direction and demonstrated His awesome power. Now at this moment of crisis, God expected Moses to know what to do: "Why are you crying out to Me...move on!"

We must diligently seek His will in stillness and prepare our life to follow where He leads; "be still and know that He is God" (Psalm 46:10). But we cannot allow our stillness to make us immobile: "Whoever watches the wind will not plant; whoever looks at the clouds will not reap" (Ecclesiastes 11:4). The conditions will never feel perfect nor will we ever feel fully prepared (beware of a never-ending mission analysis). In the end we must remember: "If God is for us, who can be against us?" (Romans 8:31).

There will always come a time when God expects us to demonstrate our faith in what He has provided. Let's prepare for that time by drawing near and learning to trust in HIS ability. Let's live with an active faith such that when we know His power, know His provision and know His direction, we are able to trust and move on.

HOLD UP THEIR ARMS

A short while after Moses and the people of Israel miraculously passed through the Red Sea, "the Amalekites came and attacked the Israelites" (Exodus 17:8). The Israelites did not have the power to win this battle on their own, so Moses sent Joshua to the battlefield and then climbed to the top of a hill: "I will stand on top of the hill with the staff of God in my hands" (Exodus 17:9).

God had previously demonstrated His power as Moses raised his staff to part the Red Sea (Exodus 14:16). He had also told Moses to use the staff to cause water to flow out of a rock (Exodus 17:5-6). Moses was now trusting God to demonstrate His power once again as he lifted this staff in battle.

Exodus 17:11-13

"As long as Moses held up his hands, the Israelites were winning, but whenever he lowered his hands, the Amalekites were winning. When Moses' hands grew tired, they took a stone and put it under him and he sat on it. Aaron and Hur held his hands up - one on one side, one on the other - so that his hands remained steady till sunset. So Joshua overcame the Amalekite army with the sword."

Moses knew what he had to do, but he simply became worn out. Fortunately for the people of Israel, Moses had two trusted companions who stood by his side and were willing to hold up his arms until the battle was won.

Many people have committed their lives to fighting the battle for the Kingdom of God. These, who are daily on the front lines, feel greatly outnumbered and are prone to grow weary. They desperately need an Aaron and a Hur to come alongside with prayer and encouragement.

I feel very fortunate to have people all over the world praying for this ministry. Almost every day I receive notes saying "Thank you" and encouraging me to continue. This is a wonderful blessing and a confirmation that we are on the right path!

Our pastors, ministry leaders, missionaries, and those who continually look for ways to serve, need this same type of support; "Encourage one another daily, as long as it is called Today, so that none of you may be hardened by sin's deceitfulness" (Hebrews 3:13). Those who faithfully serve may appear strong and confident, but their arms are getting very tired and they need to be reassured. Our missionaries have stepped out with great faith, but they are also very lonely and need to know someone still cares.

Many of our Brothers and Sisters are on the front lines of battle today. Let's join them by becoming a continual "supply line" of encouragement and prayer. Let's be like Aaron and Hur, and hold up their arms!

WATCH FOR HIS RETURN

There will always be a fascination with the end times. There will be those who study every detail of scripture in an attempt to pinpoint a date and those who simply believe the end is near because of our current moral decay. Debates will continue about when Christ will return for His Church and exactly what signs will precede this wonderful event. Unfortunately, these debates often become heated and turn our attention away from the One who has promised to return.

Questions concerning the end times are not new. Two thousand years ago, the disciples asked Jesus: "What will be the signs of Your coming and of the end of the age?" (Matthew 24:3). Jesus answered the question directly and in several parables, but His basic message was: "You also must be ready, because the Son of Man will come at an hour when you do not expect Him" (Matthew 24:44).

There's nothing fundamentally wrong with discussing the end times. The return of Jesus Christ is our "blessed hope" (Titus 2:13). We are encouraged to live as those "who have longed for His appearing" (2 Timothy 4:8). But we should never allow our discussions to lead us into "foolish and stupid arguments" (2 Timothy 2:23). Though the scholars may not agree about the details, one fact is unanimously proclaimed: "He's coming back!"

Mark 13:35-37

"Therefore keep watch because you do not know when the owner of the house will come back - whether in the evening, or at midnight, or when the rooster crows, or at dawn. If he comes suddenly, do not let him find you sleeping. What I say to you, I say to everyone: 'Watch!'"

Are we ready for the Owner of the House to return? We can't afford to wait for that next promotion or for the kids to grow - we must wake up and be prepared today. We can't wait for our house to be built to our satisfaction before we dedicate it to the service of the Lord...we must give Him our all and serve Him today.

If the end of our time on earth were to occur tomorrow, did our thoughts, words, and deeds for today bring glory and honor to our Heavenly Father? If the answer is no, we need to do some changing - we need to arise from our Spiritual slumber and clean house. For what is the purpose of our being allowed to walk this earth if not to bring Him glory?

The study and discussion of end times should cause us to praise God for His victory over evil. Our understanding of the end times should cause us to walk in reverent obedience and help us to fight the pulls of the world. Let's not be caught sleeping. Rather, let's look forward with great anticipation and commit to being prepared. Let's draw near to God in all we do and watch for His return.

SET THE EXAMPLE

When Paul wrote to the Corinthians, the gospel accounts of Jesus had not yet been written. Most believers didn't know many details of Jesus' life, so it was difficult to encourage by saying to live as Jesus would live. Instead, Paul led others to Jesus through the example he demonstrated in his own life.

1 Corinthians 11:1

"Follow my example, as I follow the example of Christ."

In setting the example, Paul certainly didn't claim to be perfect. He would be the first to stand up and say; "What a wretched man I am!" (Romans 7:24). Though Paul wrote and preached on how to live the Christian life, he still admitted his imperfections; "Not that I have already obtained all this, or have been made perfect, but I press on to take hold of that which Christ Jesus took hold of me" (Philippians 3:12).

And yet, Paul also knew he was a child of God and was willing to place his life in open view for others to examine and imitate; "Whatever you have learned or received or heard from me, or seen in me - put it into practice" (Philippians 4:9).

When we claim to follow Jesus, the world takes notice - whether we like it or not. We may not feel we are witnessing, but for many people we're the only view of Jesus they will ever see and the only words of Jesus they will ever hear. We may not realize it, but the way we live cries out: "Follow my example, as I follow the example of Christ."

Do we want others to put into practice what they see in us? Would our example cause others to be drawn closer to God or to drift further away? Do we follow Jesus' command to love one another so that, "By this all men will know you are My disciples" (John 13:35). This is a huge responsibility and one we must not assume is only for the "Super-Christian."

A good friend of mine had an "I Love Jesus" sticker on his car. One day, as he sped in and out of traffic, he realized his driving was not setting a good Christian example. He solved this "problem" by removing the sticker. Rather than modify an area of his life, my friend removed his public identification with Jesus; this is very sad!

We cannot remove the "I Love Jesus" stickers from our life. The world is watching and we must be bold enough to stand and accept the accountability. We need men and women of strength and character - Brothers and Sisters who love one another and love the Lord with all their heart, soul, mind, and strength! I urge you to be among those who commit to live a life that brings glory and honor to God in ALL you do. Others are ready to follow. Let's be bold and direct them to Christ as we set the example.

LOOKING AT OUR HEART

After Joshua died, the nation of Israel was ruled by judges for over 300 years. During this time, the people turned to God when life became difficult, but "did evil in the eyes of the Lord" (Judges 3:7) when the difficult times passed. Finally, they cried out for a king: "We want a king to rule us. Then we will be like the other nations" (1 Samuel 8:20). God gave them exactly what they wanted - He gave them Saul, "An impressive young man without equal among the Israelites" (1 Samuel 9:2).

Saul looked impressive and was loved by the people, but he failed to obey God's commands. After several years, God rejected Saul as king and sent Samuel to anoint a new king from among the sons of Jesse. When Samuel arrived at Jesse's home, he saw Eliab and thought for sure he was to be the next king (Eliab was probably tall and strong like Saul).

1 Samuel 16:7

"But the Lord said to Samuel, 'Do not consider his appearance or his height, for I have rejected him. The Lord does not look at the things man looks at. Man looks at the outward appearance, but the Lord looks at the heart.'"

Samuel assumed the next king would fit the same "impressive" mold as Saul. But this king was to be chosen according to the criteria of God, not the criteria of man. God chose David, not because of his appearance or status, but because of his heart.

How often do we fall into the trap of evaluating others based on outward appearance? We drift toward the "normal" crowd and wrongly assume that, somehow, good looks and status produce wisdom. But God calls us to consider the heart of others and to strongly consider the condition of our own heart!

Much of our life is focused on being externally impressive. We desire the "right" looks, credentials, and possessions. We believe our outward condition makes us more acceptable, but God looks past the external and directly pierces into who we are on the inside. Our focus must forever be on how we are viewed in the eyes of God, not the eyes of man.

There are very few things with eternal value. And NOTHING outside the will of God can survive the flames of judgment. The priorities of our life become the treasures which mold our heart; "Where your treasure is, there your heart will be also" (Matthew 6:21). And our heart is NEVER hidden from the eyes of God!

Let's keep our treasure firmly in the Hands of God. Let's begin to consider the riches stored inside our Brothers and Sisters, and consider our true appearance as we stand before our holy Father. Everything external will one day fade away and we will stand bare, empty handed, with God looking at our heart.

CARRY US TO COMPLETION

A great tragedy within the Christian faith is that many who believe they are on their way to Heaven will one day find they are sadly mistaken. They have been misled into believing that Church membership or good deeds will insure Salvation, but they will be cast aside on the day of judgement. This tragedy must be fought by speaking the truth about Salvation. We must teach of the need to trust in the saving grace offered through the sacrifice of Jesus for the forgiveness of sin. We must teach that faith in Jesus Christ - the Lord and Savior clearly presented in God's Word - is the ONLY way!

A second tragedy is that many who have truly trusted in Jesus for the forgiveness of sin, and desire to love Him and serve Him with all their heart, will live their days full of doubt and fear. They are on their way to Heaven but doubt when they don't feel "good enough" to deserve such a gift, and they fear a Holy God who couldn't possibly save such a wretched sinner. As they draw closer to the Light, their failures are revealed and they become discouraged or try to "work" harder to please God and gain His acceptance. We must also fight this tragedy by speaking the truth about Salvation.

The glorious truth is that none of us are good enough! "For all have sinned and fall short of the glory of God" (Romans 3:23). Without God's grace, no one can ever hope to hit the mark of His perfect glory.

We don't enter Heaven based on what we've done, but only on whom we've placed our faith; "For it is by grace you have been saved, through faith" (Ephesians 2:8). At the moment of Salvation, we become an eternal Child of God: "You are not your own; you were bought at a price" (1 Corinthians 6:19-20). We were purchased with His blood and have become a "new creation: the old has gone, the new has come" (2 Corinthians 5:17). A new creation does not continue down the same path.

We are "born again" when the Spirit of God transforms our heart; and as a new creation, we must learn to crawl, then walk, and one day run! We may stumble, but God promises we will continue to grow; for it's His plan that ALL His children become "conformed to the likeness of His Son" (Romans 8:29), and being conformed is a lifetime process!

Philippians 1:6

"Being confident of this, that He who began a good work in you will carry it on to completion until the day of Christ Jesus."

God has given us His Holy Spirit and "sealed {us} for the day of redemption" (Ephesians 4:30). Let's be confident in God's promise. We must continue to draw closer and give Him more of our heart, but we must also remember that we are His and He WILL finish the work He began. Our Heavenly Father has saved us AND promised to carry us to completion.

THEIR FIELD OF PIGS

The parable of the prodigal son has had special meaning to our family over the last several years. We've witnessed nearly every aspect of this parable work itself out through the life of our daughter, from the pain of her rebellion to the joy of her return. I've also seen this as the most common problem faced by parents all over the world. No matter what country or culture, parents agonize over the one who has gone astray.

In this parable, we see a rebellious young man demanding what he felt was rightfully his: "Father, give me my share of the estate" (Luke 15:12). This disrespectful attitude grew until the son no longer desired to live under his father's roof. He "got together all he had, set off for a distant country and there squandered his wealth in wild living" (Luke 15:13).

The reason this is such a universally common issue is that we are all born with the same sinful nature - a nature which holds us in tight control unless we are utterly transformed by the Spirit of God through faith in Jesus. "Those who live according to the sinful nature have their minds set on what that nature desires" (Romans 8:5). At the heart of the sinful nature is a pride which continually demands what we believe we deserve - this is the root of all sin!

63

The prodigal son continued to live according to his sinful nature until he found himself in a field of pigs; "he longed to fill his stomach with the pods {they} were eating" (Luke 15:16). But God used this terrible situation to soften the heart of the prodigal son and bring him to a state of submitted repentance.

Luke 15:17-18

"When he came to his senses, he said, 'How many of my father's hired men have food to spare, and here I am starving to death! I will set out and go back to my father and say to him: Father, I have sinned against heaven and against you.'"

Before the son left home, I'm sure the father tried to provide wise counsel about the true priorities in life. I'm sure the father desperately tried every possible method of guiding the son along the straight and narrow path. I'm also pretty sure the father simply held his son close and wept. Unfortunately, the lessons the son needed to learn could only be taught through pigs.

There is nothing more painful than to watch someone you love walk down a path of obvious pain - nothing rips the heart like watching your child walk away from God and engage in various forms of "wild living." But it helps to remember that God loves the prodigal more than we can hope or imagine. He desires to live with them in an eternally restored relationship. Our Heavenly Father will never miss an opportunity to teach the prodigal and draw them near - even as they may drift and sink - even as they may wallow in their field of pigs.

LOVE ENOUGH TO LET GO

In the message "Their Field of Pigs" we considered the parable of the prodigal son and were encouraged to remember that God will use every tool available (even pigs) to draw His children Home. It must be our highest desire for our children, to see them secure in the arms of God. Notice that in this parable there's no mention of the father between the time the son left and when he returned home. The father appears to have watched his son leave and then simply waited for his return.

The father must have known of his son's condition while away; "this son of mine was dead and is alive again" (Luke 15:24). There must have been many reports of the son's activities which were openly discussed with the rest of the family: "The older brother became angry...'this son of yours who has squandered your property with prostitutes comes home'" (Luke 15:28,30). And yet, while the son was away, the father never once stepped in to "rescue" him.

Was the father lazy and uncaring? Was this simply the product of a macho culture that didn't show much emotion? Or was this a father who knew how God's grace could work a difficult situation toward a wonderful good?

James 1:2-4

"Consider it pure joy, my brothers, whenever you face trials of many kinds, because you know that the testing of your faith develops perseverance. Perseverance must finish its work so that you may be mature and complete, not lacking anything."

We often reference this passage during times of personal trial. These verses encourage us to understand the purpose of our difficult times and to trust God so fully that we actually rejoice because we know He is using our trials to make us complete.

Many of us understand and at least try to apply these verses in our own life. But it's an additional step of faith (a very big step) to trust and apply these verses in the life of others - especially those we dearly love. If we are to rejoice in our own trials because of the good being worked within us, there is also a sense in which we should rejoice in the trials of others.

As painful as it must have been, the father allowed God to complete His work - even though it meant his son would actually long to eat with the pigs! And yes, this father loved his son.

When someone we love goes astray, let's continue to lift them up in prayer; always let them know they are loved and continually speak a gentle message of truth. Let's NEVER give up hope, but let's allow God to finish the glorious work He's begun. Let's trust Him above ALL else and love enough to let go.

A LONG WAY OFF

In the last two messages, we've considered the parable of the prodigal son. We've seen how we must often "Love Enough to Let Go" and trust that God will continue to work in the life of our prodigal even as they walk through "Their Field of Pigs."

As the son was longing to eat the pig food, he decided to return home and began to rehearse what he would say; "I will set out and go back to my father and say to him: Father, I have sinned against heaven and against you. I am no longer worthy to be called your son" (Luke 15:18-19).

The son returned home. But before he could give his speech; before he could tell his father about eating with the pigs; before he could "prove" his repentance or say ANYTHING, the father received him with joy.

Luke 15:20

"But while he was still a long way off, his father saw him and was filled with compassion for him; he ran to his son, threw his arms around him and kissed him."

When the father saw his son had returned, he was overjoyed and wanted to celebrate: "Bring the fatted calf...for this son of mine was dead and is alive again; he was lost and is found"

(Luke 15:23,24). This type of love and joy cannot be manufactured for a one-time event, it must be established in the relationship long before there is trouble - and maintained even when all else is falling apart.

The scripture isn't clear about what turmoil occurred when the prodigal son left home. We're never told of the father's pain - but I assure you it was there. It's not clear how long the son was away - but I KNOW the father spent many anxious moments worrying about his son. And yet, when the son returned, there was joy and forgiveness. Without condoning the poor choices the son had made, the father received the son and loved him without reservation.

When we turn to our Heavenly Father in faith, He accepts us without requiring that we earn His love or demonstrate our worth. We may have drifted far away and are unsure how to find our way back into His loving arms; but when we turn and seek Him, we find He is right there ready to receive us Home.

Jesus Christ submitted to a horrible death in order to provide a path of restoration. We who have been restored are now called to restore with others in this same manner; "Forgive as the Lord forgave you" (Colossians 3:13). We are called to be a catalyst of restoration, not a hedge of thorns which must be vaulted over. When our prodigal begins to return, let's believe the best, be filled with compassion, and receive them back with true forgiveness and joy - even while they are a long way off.

THE OTHER SON

The parable of the prodigal son contains so many practical lessons on relationships (particularly for parents) that we often forget Jesus spoke this parable in response to an accusation from the Pharisees; "This man welcomes sinners and eats with them" (Luke 15:2). The message of the prodigal son is really about our Heavenly Father who rejoices every time a "sinner" turns their heart to Him in repentance. But why did Jesus talk about TWO sons? What was the message of the son who remained at home?

He was the son who quietly watched his younger brother make disrespectful demands on his father; "Give me my share of the estate" (Luke 15:12). He was the son who stayed at home to work the fields while his brother "squandered his wealth in wild living" (Luke 15:13). And he was the son who became angry with his father and refused to celebrate his brother's return: "All these years I've been slaving for you and never disobeyed your orders. Yet you never gave me even a young goat" (Luke 15:29).

This was the son who walked the straight and narrow - walked the path of disciplined obedience - but he missed his opportunity to receive true blessings as he walked.

Luke 15:31

"'My son,' the father said, 'you are always with me, and everything I have is yours.'"

The son had been "slaving" in the hope of a future blessing. But his heart was not joyfully serving, and he missed the real blessing of walking with his father and having free access to everything his father owned.

As believers in the saving grace of Jesus Christ, we understand that people can be saved at any point in their life - regardless of past sins. The thief on the cross received his Salvation only moments before he died. But there is always part of us that cries "foul!" Somehow it doesn't seem fair when others have worked so hard for so long.

This attitude shows we also have missed the blessing of walking with our Lord. Heaven is never a reward for "obedient" living; it is a free gift to those who believe in Jesus. We should never feel we're "slaving" under the burden of His commands in order to earn His favor. Rather, we are to joyfully follow because we know that only in Him is there true peace, true contentment...true blessings!

Let's follow our Lord with a firm perspective of eternity; but let's never become so focused on the future that we miss the blessings given to us today - the blessings of the journey! Let's renew our joy at being allowed to walk every day with our Heavenly Father and rejoice whenever a repentant heart returns home. Let's never make the sad mistake of living the burdened life of the other son.

CUT THE LIFEBOATS

At the end of his third missionary journey, Paul was arrested in Jerusalem, transferred about 40 miles up the road to Caesarea, and sat in prison for over two years before being sent by boat to stand trial in Rome. During the journey to Rome, a storm blew the ship off course and threatened to kill everyone on board.

Acts 27:30-32

> *"In an attempt to escape from the ship, the sailors let the lifeboat down into the sea, pretending they were going to lower some anchors from the bow. Then Paul said to the centurion and the soldiers, 'Unless these men stay with the ship, you cannot be saved.' So the soldiers cut the ropes that held the lifeboat and let it fall away."*

Where is our true security? Most of us have lifeboats which we keep close to our side. Even after we've accepted the forgiveness and saving grace of Jesus, we tend to keep the lifeboats - just in case. We say we're trusting our future to God, but we still make sure every step of our life is planned for the next 30 years and fight any attempt to deviate from "the plan" - just in case.

We say we understand the concept of eternity and the idea that our life is "a mist that appears for a little while and then vanishes" (James 4:14), but we still strive for titles and positions so our friends and family can remember us as "successful" - just in case. We say we want to live for Jesus and praise our Heavenly Father for all eternity, but we still don't want to miss the immediate pleasures of the world - just in case.

If we keep one foot in the ship and one foot in the lifeboat, we will never live as God desires. It makes absolutely no sense to say we believe and trust God with our eternity and yet fail to trust Him with the uncertainties of tomorrow or the storms of today. Cutting the lifeboats means we place ALL our trust in God, believe His Word as truth, and live accordingly: "Do not merely listen to the Word, and so deceive yourselves. Do what it says" (James 1:22).

We MUST stay with the ship! A saving relationship with Jesus implies we have recognized the eternal storm of sin which threatened to sink us to the pit of hell, but it also implies we are clinging to His forgiveness as the ONLY way to be saved; "for there is no other name under Heaven given to men by which we must be saved" (Acts 4:12).

Let's ask the Holy Spirit to reveal any area of our life which is not consistent with a life of unrestrained belief and trust. Then, let's ask for the strength and courage to, once and for all, give Him ALL of our heart and cut the lifeboats.

THE FATHER'S VIEW

In the message "Cut The Lifeboats" we were encouraged to cut away those areas of our life which still cling to the world's answers for fulfillment and security - those areas which keep our hearts from being fully devoted to God. But at the same time, we acknowledged this can be a difficult process. One reason for this difficulty is our extremely limited view of our life and the world around us.

Our flawed perception is not unlike a tiny ant. These small creatures seem to never stop working as they scurry about frantically moving little grains of sand from here to there in the hope of building a secure home. If we could ask an ant to describe his world, he might tell us about his hole in the ground, about the few thousand members of his family, and maybe something about the few surrounding meters where he gathers food. Obviously, the ant has a very limited view of the real world.

But as our Heavenly Father watches us build our homes of security - watches us frantically moving from here to there, trying to climb to the top of the hill - He also sees a creation with a VERY limited view of the real world; "As the heavens are higher than the earth, so are My ways higher than your ways and My thoughts than your thoughts" (Isaiah 55:9).

As seen from God's perspective, we have almost no understanding of how the little corner of our life fits into His plan or how our current problems are leading us closer to Him. From God's perspective our view is as limited as the ant. But, though we may not fully see or understand, He is calling us to trust.

Proverbs 3:5-6

"Trust in the Lord with all your heart and lean not on your own understanding; in all your ways acknowledge Him, and He will make your paths straight."

Many of us are facing difficult circumstances. We want to walk along God's path and live a life pleasing to Him, but we're not sure which direction to turn. Our indecision is often because we only trust in what we clearly understand - and we've begun to realize our understanding is not very clear. But God's promise is that as we love and trust Him with all our heart, the path directly in front of us will become straight - as we trust, the decisions will become clear and we will KNOW our next step!

We must truly believe that our Heavenly Father sees and hears ALL, and that He's infinitely complete in understanding. Where we are fortunate to see a few short steps down the path, He sees the entire journey - the journey leading us "to be conformed to the likeness of His Son" (Romans 8:29), and the destination of spending all eternity praising His name. We must keep stepping out in faith, but we must do so by leaning on Him, continually seeking His direction, and trusting the Father's view.

HE CHOSE TO DIE

The Passion of The Christ opened on February 25th, 2004 in 2800 movie theaters across the US and I'm certain will soon be seen in every country where it's not expressly forbidden. I highly recommend this movie for any Christians (or at least those with an understanding of the gospel message) who are mature enough to watch and comprehend the significance of the graphic violence of crucifixion.

If you view this movie, please understand that every depiction of humiliation and pain was true. But also understand that every drop of blood shed by Jesus was by choice according to the predetermined plan of God. The gospel is a message of a loving Savior who willingly gave Himself so we could live. A sacrifice for sin has always been required, but Jesus became the final and everlasting sacrifice.

Hebrews 9:13-14

"The blood of goats and bulls and the ashes of a heifer sprinkled on those who are ceremonially unclean sanctify them so that they are outwardly clean. How much more, then, will the blood of Christ, who through the eternal Spirit offered Himself unblemished to God, cleanse our consciences from acts that lead to death, so that we may serve the living God!"

Most of the discussion leading up to this movie has been focused on how it may cause persecution against the Jews around the world. It's a VERY sad truth, but for almost two thousand years misguided and ignorant people have caused great harm in the name of Christ. Such actions reveal a lack of basic Biblical understanding. Jesus GAVE His life, no one took it! And He did so for our sin...MY sin!! My sin sent Jesus to the cross, and He willingly surrendered His life because He loves me: "You see, at just the right time, when we were still powerless, Christ died for the ungodly... But God demonstrates His own love for us in this: While we were still sinners, Christ died for us" (Romans 5:6,8).

The damage done over the years affects how the gospel message is received today. Many groups need to know the saving love of Jesus, but maybe they first need to know that a Christian knows how to love. Father, forgive us for the barriers we've erected and for those we've kept from knowing Your Son.

I pray that many lives will be forever changed by the viewing of this movie. I pray we can see the true love story of a Father who gave His Son, and a Son who gave His life. Every detail was planned before the beginning of time; "This man was handed over to you by God's set purpose and foreknowledge" (Acts 2:23). His death was horrific in order to demonstrate the ugliness of sin and the extent of His love. He walked every painful step so we could be united with the Father for all eternity. He surrendered Himself to the cross because He loves us so much that He chose to die.

FREE OF THORNS

In the parable of the sower (Matthew 13:3-8), Jesus tells about a farmer who scatters seed on four different types of soil: packed, shallow, thorny, and fertile. In this parable, the seed refers to the Word of God and the soil refers to those who hear the Word.

Those of packed soil have hearts which are so hard that they immediately turn away. Those of shallow soil may quickly germinate and grow, but they also quickly lose interest and die. Most of us reading this type of message fall into one of the last two types of soil. We desire God's Word to grow on the fertile ground of our heart and produce a bountiful crop, but we seem to continually battle the thorns.

Matthew 13:22

"The one who received the seed that fell among the thorns is the man who hears the Word, but the worries of this life and the deceitfulness of wealth choke it, making it unfruitful."

We have more opportunity to receive God's Word today than any other time in history. We can hear good preaching in church, on radio, on tape, or even over the internet. We can read God's Word in a variety of translations and receive an abundance of help with interpretation. Our soil is definitely receiving seed. But the challenge is to keep our lives free of the distractions which hinder growth.

Here's a simple test of our soil. Jesus said the number one commandment is to "Love the Lord your God with all your heart and with all your soul and with all your mind" (Matthew 22:37). When was the last time our heart overflowed with love for God? When was the last time we considered the sacrifice of Jesus and nearly bubbled over with "Thank You!"?

God desires for us to love Him. In fact, His entire Word is a message of calling us back to a loving relationship. If we have a hard time following His most basic desire, it's no wonder we're confused about where He's leading. We look for specific direction with where to live and work, yet we fail to give Him the entirety of our heart and simply worship at His feet.

When God's Word comes into our life, we should receive it and cherish it as a precious gift. We ought to immediately look for ways to apply His Word and make it grow, not process it through the distractions of deadlines, appointments, bills, and worldly relationships and ambitions.

Is the Word growing in our life, or is it being choked by unnecessary demands of the world? "The world and its desires pass away" (1 John 2:17), but the things of God are eternal. He is calling us to live a life fully dedicated to Him in ALL we do. Let's weed our garden and remove distractions so the seed of His Word can grow and bear fruit. Let's begin to develop fertile soil which is free of thorns.

ALWAYS REJOICE

In his letter to the Philippians, Paul gives an exhortation to "Rejoice in the Lord always - and again I say, rejoice!" (Philippians 4:4). Paul had been arrested and sent to Rome to await trial. He spent his days and nights under house arrest chained to a Roman soldier, but was still able to say, rejoice...always!

When we begin to understand the life changing gift of forgiveness through faith in the sacrifice of Jesus - when we truly grasp the concept of eternity and, through faith, believe we will spend all eternity in the presence of God - we have more than enough reason to rejoice, no matter what our present circumstances might be.

If we are unable to rejoice, we have allowed our eyes to become too fixed on the present. Our attention has become focused on our earthly desires, goals and ambitions, and we have lost sight of the blessings of a life in Christ. Either that, or we don't really believe!

The verses which immediately follow Paul's call to rejoice list some real benefits of a life of rejoicing.

Philippians 4:5-7

"Let your gentleness be evident to all. The Lord is near. Do not be anxious about

anything, but in everything, by prayer and petition, with thanksgiving, present your requests to God. And the peace of God, which transcends all understanding, will guard your hearts and your minds in Christ Jesus."

Gentleness and a lack of anxiety result from rejoicing in a risen Savior. If Jesus Christ can be raised from the dead and sit down "at the right hand of God" (Hebrews 10:12), then our Heavenly Father can certainly take care of problems with our job, health, kids, finances or relationships - so rejoice! When we rejoice and focus on an eternity in Heaven and a Savior who walks by our side, our anxiety fades - our present trials become "light and momentary" (2 Corinthians 4:17).

When we live a life filled with rejoicing, we are able to focus on the solutions we know God can provide. We develop a heart of thanksgiving - a heart which naturally presents everything to God in prayer and waits with grateful expectation for His reply. We begin to trust in God's plan for our life and His desire for us to be with Him forever. The result, which admittedly takes time and patience, is "the peace of God which transcends all understanding."

These words written by Paul are not the deluded ramblings of an old man in Roman confinement, they are the true promises of God! They represent a promised life we all can live. Our Father offers us a life of gentleness, contentment, and peace; a life free of anxiety and worry. But this life can only happen if we love and trust Him with all our heart, and if we are determined to always rejoice.

OPPORTUNITY OF OUR WORDS

Every day we are given the opportunity to make a difference in someone's life. Every time we open our mouth to speak, we send forth words which have an effect on those around us. Our words, which come "out of the overflow of the heart" (Matthew 12:34), will either cause a positive or negative reaction - our word are rarely neutral. Knowing the power of our words ought to cause us to use them with great care.

Ephesians 4:29

"Do not let any unwholesome talk come out of your mouths, but only what is helpful for building others up according to their needs, that it may benefit those who listen."

This means that every time we speak, we have the opportunity to encourage and minister. With just a few moments of our time and very little effort, we have the opportunity to brighten someone's day, to ease their burden, and possibly draw them closer to God. This precious opportunity must not be taken lightly; "But I tell you that men will have to give account on the day of judgment for every careless word they have spoken" (Matthew 12:26).

Though our careless words are eternally forgiven, they are also a reflection of our heart. If we have received Jesus as our Lord and Savior, our heart ought to be filled with devotion, and our words should be filtered through a desire to bring Him glory and honor. I'm afraid we will one day be deeply ashamed to see how much damage our words have caused.

We seldom realize how harmful and discouraging our words can be: "Like a madman shooting firebrands or deadly arrows is a man who deceives his neighbor and says, 'I was only joking!'" (Proverbs 26:18-19). Sarcastic and joking words are "deadly arrows" which are never useful for "building others up." Over time, this mode of communication is sure to destroy a relationship.

Before we speak, we must carefully listen. What is the real question? What are the real needs? "He who answers before listening - that is his folly and his shame" (Proverbs 18:13). We may only be given the opportunity to speak a few words, but we can make every effort to use our words wisely; "The heart of the righteous weighs its answers, but the mouth of the wicked gushes evil" (Proverbs 15:28).

Our words are a powerful gift. Let's honor our Heavenly Father by effectively using this gift to encourage. Let's speak so those who listen may benefit and be built up in their faith. Let's continually encourage one another to draw closer to our Heavenly Father and never squander the opportunity of our words.

DEDICATE HIS TEMPLE

The Old Testament adds wonderful richness to our faith. In the very first verse of the Bible we read "God created the heavens and the earth" (Genesis 1:1). By reflecting on this wonderful truth we can better understand the words of Jesus that "with God all things are possible" (Matthew 19:26). Throughout the Old Testament we see God use common people to accomplish His plan and point the way to Christ. We also learn to appreciate the purpose of a life of absolute reverence for God.

After the Israelites were led out of Egypt, God gave instructions to Moses for constructing the Tabernacle. This was to be the central place of worship and where the presence of God would reside. It was made of cloth, animal skins and poles, so it could be easily moved.

After several hundred years, the people of Israel settled into the promised land and God gave King David the vision for a permanent Temple to replace the mobile Tabernacle. David made plans and collected material, but God waited for Solomon to become king before construction began.

It took Solomon seven years to construct the Temple using over 150,000 workers (2 Chronicles 2:1-2). When the Temple was complete, the dedication began. Sacrifices were made to honor and worship God. Music was played and songs were sung "to give praise and thanks to the Lord" (2 Chronicles 5:13). The grand dedication said that this was to be a place to honor God forevermore!

2 Chronicles 5:13-14

> *"Then the Temple of the Lord was filled with a cloud, and the priests could not perform their service because of the cloud, for the glory of the Lord filled the Temple of God."*

The purpose of the Temple was to lead the children of Israel to a closer relationship with God through an understanding of sin, sacrifice, forgiveness and worship. It was also designed to lead them toward Jesus and provide us with an understanding of who we are in Christ.

One thousand years after the Temple was dedicated, Jesus died on the cross and we entered into a new covenant with a new Temple; "Don't you know that you yourselves are God's Temple and that God's Spirit lives in you?" (1 Corinthians 3:16). When we enter into a covenant relationship with God through faith in Jesus Christ, we become the Temple of God. He now resides in the heart of every believer.

The Old Testament shows us the great honor and responsibility of being God's Temple. He resides in us and we must be so filled with the glory of the Lord that we no longer perform "our" service but glorify His name in all we do. Let's set aside the entirety of our life as a holy place of worship...forevermore! Let's give praise and thanks to the Lord and begin today to dedicate His Temple.

EVER-INCREASING GLORY

In the message "Dedicate His Temple" we saw that through the forgiveness of Jesus and the indwelling of the Holy Spirit, we are now God's Temple; "Don't you know that you yourselves are God's Temple and that God's Spirit lives in you?" (1 Corinthians 3:16). And as with the Temple during the reign of King Solomon, we are to dedicate ourselves for worship and be filled with His glory (2 Chronicles 5:13-14).

The glory of the Lord first appeared to the people of Israel after they were led out of Egypt; "They looked toward the desert, and there was the glory of the Lord appearing in the cloud" (Exodus 16:10). Then, when Moses was called up Mount Sinai to receive the law, the glory of the Lord settled over the mountain; "To the Israelites the glory of the Lord looked like a consuming fire" (Exodus 24:17).

When Moses came down from the mountain, "his face was radiant because he had spoken with the Lord" (Exodus 34:29). The presence of God did not cause Moses' face to simply shine with a joyful glow, it beamed with a fear-causing glory; "When Aaron and all the Israelites saw Moses, his face was radiant, and they were afraid to come near him" (Exodus 34:30). After Moses spoke to the people, he "put a veil over his face" (Exodus 34:33) to ease their fear as well as cover the fact that "the radiance was fading away" (2 Corinthians 3:13).

These examples of God's glory give us a sense of awe. God's glory reflects His character - His majesty, holiness, and awesome power. As believers in Jesus Christ, we are now God's Temple and "ministers of a new covenant" (2 Corinthians 3:6). We are no longer like Moses who had to cover his face with a veil. Jesus has removed the veil and we can boldly reflect His glory into a lost and dying world.

2 Corinthians 3:18

"And we, who with unveiled faces all reflect the Lord's glory, are being transformed into His likeness with ever-increasing glory."

When we accept Jesus as our Lord and Savior, we reflect the glory of the Lord from within as we are transformed into the image of Christ. This transformation produces a glory which is intended to increase for the rest of our days. We will never attain the full likeness of Christ until we join Him in Heaven; but, with every step along God's path, we become more and more like His Son. And as the radiant-blocking "self" is slowly removed, we are better able to reflect His glory.

We must continue down His path. We must take daily steps toward a life which reflects the glory of the Lord into the darkness that surrounds us. Heavenly Father, we pray for the strength to more fully surrender and reflect You into this world with an ever-increasing glory.

ENTER HIS REST

In the last two messages, we've considered the glory of the Lord. We saw how we are now God's Temple and are to "reflect the Lord's glory" (2 Corinthians 3:18) into the world as we are transformed into the likeness of Christ. It is a great honor to be in the presence of the Lord and we have been given the awesome responsibility to reflect an "ever-increasing" amount of His glory.

But what does this really mean? How can we increase the glory our life reflects?

When we place our life in the Hands of God through faith in Jesus Christ, we are given His Spirit "with whom you were sealed for the day of redemption" (Ephesians 4:30). We reflect His glory as we submit to His leading and allow the fruit of His Spirit to be evident in our life; "the fruit of the Spirit is love, joy, peace, patience, kindness, goodness, faithfulness, gentleness and self-control" (Galatians 5:22-23). As we further submit and allow His fruit to define the character of our life, God's glory will shine!

Notice that the focus of reflecting His glory is on submission, not on our effort. When the glory of the Lord filled Solomon's Temple, "the priests could not perform their service" (2 Chronicles 5:14). God's glory and the work we perform through our own effort are incompatible.

Hebrews 4:10-11

"For anyone who enters God's rest also rests from his own work, just as God did from His. Let us, therefore, make every effort to enter that rest."

God created the heavens and the earth in six days; "By the seventh day God had finished the work He had been doing; so on the seventh day he rested from all His work" (Genesis 2:2). God was satisfied with His work and entered His rest for all eternity. He is still intimately involved, but God accomplishes everything from a confident and calm position of rest because He KNOWS the final outcome.

Likewise, we must not cease from doing the things God calls us to do, but we must cease from working in our own strength and for our own self-righteous rewards. God will certainly keep us active, but the focus of our effort must be on serving and growing from a position of rest with a true desire to do ALL for the love of God.

Many of us are attempting to walk His path in our own strength by working hard and carrying the burdens which are rightfully His. This is not our call! We must love Him with all our heart and serve Him with all our strength. But we must do so through joyful surrender, daily submission and obedience. He will accomplish His work in His time and according to His purpose. Let's continue to reflect more and more of His glory. Let's draw closer into His presence and make every effort to enter His rest.

STRONG, COURAGEOUS, AND HUMBLE

Joshua was Moses' field commander in the fight against the Amalekites (Exodus 17:9) and his assistant when the Law was given at Mount Sinai (Exodus 24:13). After initially exploring the land of Canaan, Joshua was one of only two men to advise the Israelites to trust God and enter the promised land (Numbers 14:6-9). When the people refused, Joshua received an additional 39 years of leadership training from Moses while the Israelites were led through the desert.

God then selected Joshua to succeed Moses; "At his command he and the entire community of the Israelites will go out, and at his command they will come in" (Numbers 27:21). After Moses died, God gave final instructions to Joshua before leading the people into the land of Canaan.

Joshua 1:9

"Have I not commanded you? Be strong and courageous. Do not be terrified; do not be discouraged, for the Lord your God will be with you wherever you go."

Joshua would be required to fight many battles and lead a great multitude of people, so God repeated His encouragement several times... "Be strong and courageous!"

This is an awesome exhortation for us today. God has given us His instructions, empowered us with His Spirit, and has told us to boldly proceed down His path knowing He is by our side wherever we go. But there's an additional lesson God desires all His children to learn.

Prior to his first battle in Canaan, Joshua "saw a man standing in front of him with a drawn sword in his hand" (Joshua 5:13). This caused Joshua some obvious concern, so he approached the man and asked; "Are you for us or for our enemies?"

Joshua 5:14

> "'Neither,' he replied, 'but as commander of the army of the Lord I have now come.' Then Joshua fell facedown to the ground in reverence, and asked him, 'What message does my Lord have for His servant?'"

We are called to be bold, but our boldness will always become self serving unless we totally submit to God's leadership - unless we say with complete humility: "Lord, You are the Commander and this is Your army. I will fight with courage and strength, but these are Your battles. What would You have me do, and where would You have me go?" As we boldly go forward into God's Land of Promise, our marching orders are clear: we are to always be strong, courageous, and humble.

GOD MAKES IT GROW

Paul wrote his first letter to the Corinthian church to correct several problems. The Corinthian's needed instruction in marriage, Christian freedom, worship, and various issues which tended to cause division. He rebuked the church for quarreling about whom they followed: "You are still worldly... For when one says, 'I follow Paul,' and another, 'I follow Apollos,' are you not mere men?" (1 Corinthians 3:3,4).

Apollos was a good teacher, but Paul reminds us that all ministers of the Gospel - all preachers, teachers, parents, and anyone else who desires to share Biblical truths - are simply servants through whom God accomplishes His work. We become worldly and fail to live according to the Spirit of God any time we become followers of a specific minister or feel responsible for someone's growth and maturity.

1 Corinthians 3:5-6

"What, after all, is Apollos? And what is Paul? Only servants, through whom you came to believe - as the Lord has assigned to each his task. I planted the seed, Apollos watered it, but God made it grow."

We must always remain exclusive followers of Jesus Christ! Though He may use many others to assist in the process, God must receive ALL the credit and glory for our growth. In the same manner, God uses each of us to ASSIST in the growth of others. We can teach truth with our words and demonstrate truth with our lives, but we can never cause someone to accept the truth or even grow to a deeper understanding.

We are instructed to plant the seed of His Word and water with discipleship, prayer, and encouragement at every opportunity; "We are therefore Christ's ambassadors, as though God were making His appeal through us" (2 Corinthians 5:20).

As we plant and water, it's normal to want to see some growth. We may desire to see blossoms overnight, but God is growing a mighty shade tree with deep roots and wide branches that will not break in the wind - and this kind of growth takes time. We may NEVER see the eternal results of our effort, but we must patiently continue to plant and water, and trust God to accomplish His work; "{My Word} will not return to Me empty, but will accomplish what I desire and achieve the purpose for which I have sent it" (Isaiah 55:11).

Each of us knows someone who needs to know our Heavenly Father in a more personal way. There are great ministry opportunities placed in our path every day. Let's obediently follow by being well nourished and casting forth the seed and water of His Word without becoming discouraged. Let's remember we are the servants through whom He works, but let's ALWAYS remember that God makes it grow!

CAREFUL THOUGHT TO OUR WAYS

The motivational speakers of our day want us to set great goals for our life: "Where do you want to be in two, five, or ten years? What type of lifestyle do you want when you retire?" We are encouraged to set goals slightly beyond our reach, and then instructed how to create a plan to accomplish these goals. The implication is that a more focused effort will yield superior results and lead to greater "success."

But before we can ask where we want to be in the next few years, we must first ask a longer term question: "Where will I be in one hundred years?" No other goal is worth pursuing until we have a solid answer to this most basic (but all-important) question. What difference does it make which college we attend, which job we take, or what our home looks like if we have failed to address the issue of where we will spend eternity!?

Proverbs 14:8

> *"The wisdom of the prudent is to give thought to their ways, but the folly of fools is deception."*

We must be wise with the days we are given and no longer be deceived by the values of the world's system. There's nothing inherently wrong with goals and plans, but, far too often, they lead to a self-determined lifestyle and away from the true Director of ALL plans; "In his heart a man plans his course, but the Lord determines his steps" (Proverbs 16:9). Our planning must be as a direct response to God's leading; and once in place, our plans must remain in complete submission to His will; "I know, O Lord, that a man's life is not his own; it is not for man to direct his steps" (Jeremiah 10:23).

Every moment of our life is a precious gift from God. Even though the average life span continues to increase, our time is extremely short. An average life lasts about 45,000,000 minutes (much less in many countries). This may seem like a lot, but by this time tomorrow 1440 minutes will be forever gone; "You are a mist that appears for a little while and then vanishes" (James 4:14).

We must not waste our limited time by chasing after things which vanish; "Be very careful, then, how you live - not as unwise but as wise, making the most of every opportunity" (Ephesians 5:15-16). We must evaluate ALL our decisions and goals based on the overriding desire to glorify God in all we do, to rejoice in His many blessings, and to long for the time when we can worship before His throne for all eternity. Any other set of values must fade to nothing in comparison.

Every day we are handed a block of time and given the freedom of how it will be spent. This is a wonderful opportunity, but the clock continues to tick! Let's honor our Heavenly Father with our goals and plans and give careful thought to our ways.

GREAT EXPECTATIONS

In the message "Careful Thought To Our Ways" we saw how God is the Director of our steps and how we must carefully (and prayerfully) develop goals and plans which glorify His name. And though our true goal should always be to fully release our life to God and worship Him for all eternity, each day we walk this earth can be filled with a wonderful excitement as we live for Him.

Paul was confined in Rome when he wrote his letter to the Philippians. He didn't know whether he would be set free or executed, but he knew Jesus Christ as his Lord and Savior. Paul had seen God's hand at work and fully understood His love and power. He had completely turned his life over to God and now lived with an excitement at how God would use him to accomplish His plan.

Philippians 1:20

"I eagerly expect and hope that I will in no way be ashamed, but will have sufficient courage so that now as always Christ will be exalted in my body whether by life or by death."

There were times when Paul's situation appeared dismal and without hope, but he had already seen how God was using ALL things to

His glory; "It has become clear throughout the whole palace guard and to everyone else that I am in chains for Christ" (Philippians 1:13). Paul's hardship had made it possible for the whole palace guard to hear the gospel message and had encouraged others to "speak the word of God more courageously and fearlessly" (Philippians 1:14). Paul had learned the true joy of being a vessel through whom God could work.

As we follow Jesus we must develop a view which is not constrained by what we see; "For what is seen is temporary, but what is unseen is eternal" (2 Corinthians 4:18). He is ALWAYS at work, and always inviting us to join by His side. As we develop an eternal view of this world, we will see every situation as working toward His good. Trials will become a wonderful time of growth, and interruptions in our plans will become exciting God-directed opportunities for ministry.

We spend so much time trying to create our future happiness that we miss the true joy God has for us today. He is calling us to know Him better and love Him more; to experience His love and share His love with others. He has a wonderful and exciting plan for us TODAY! "He is our God and we are the people of His pasture" (Psalm 95:7).

Let's begin each day with a wondrous anticipation: "I can't wait to see what God has for me today!" God has an amazing plan for our life! Let's develop a view which looks and longs for opportunities to draw near, love Him, and serve. Let's live each day filled with joy and great expectations.

BUILD ALL FOR HIS GLORY

The last two messages have considered how we ought to use a different set of priorities in forming our goals and plans. Our goal should be to fully submit to our Heavenly Father, and our plans must always remain under His control. We also saw that a life submitted to God is full of opportunity and excitement. But such a submitted life requires discipline and perseverance. Though the world may scream for us to return, we must be determined to continue to live by the truth of God's Word.

In 586 BC, the armies of Babylon destroyed the Temple in Jerusalem. About 50 years later, the Jewish people started to rebuild; but after a few years, their priorities began to shift. Their comfort and the condition of their own homes became more important than being obedient to God's call: "Is it time for you yourselves to be living in your paneled houses, while this house {of the Lord} remains a ruin?" (Haggai 1:4). God sent the prophet Haggai to challenge the people to reconsider their values and return to the work they had begun.

Haggai 1:5-6

"Give careful thought to your ways. You have planted much, but have harvested little. You eat, but never have enough. You drink, but never have your fill. You put

on clothes, but are not warm. You earn wages, only to put them in a purse with holes in it."

The people had turned from rebuilding the Temple to building their own homes - from rebuilding their Spiritual lives to building the comfort of their physical lives - and found that no matter how hard they worked, they never had enough. Isn't it amazing how the foundational truths never change?

We have more pulls on our priorities today than at any other time in history. There are more distractions, more temptations, and many more "construction projects" that cry for our time and energy. But if our focus remains on building for our own physical comfort and security, we will also be ones who find we are NEVER satisfied. It may take many years to realize this truth, but without an eternal focus on the glory and honor of God, all our effort drains away.

Our lives have become a Temple of God - a Temple being built to worship Him for all eternity, and one which must not fall into ruin! We must build the foundation of this Temple through intimate prayer and the study of His Word. We must cover all we build with an overriding desire to love God "with all your heart and with all your soul and with all your mind and with all your strength" (Mark 12:30).

Each and every day we are given the task of building His Spiritual Temple. Let's not be turned from this task by projects which so easily fade away. Let's refocus our priorities and diligently build ALL for His glory.

FORGIVE AS HE FORGAVE

It seems like sooner or later everyone gets mistreated and hurt. Many times the actions against us are unintentional, but other times they can be extremely malicious. Suddenly, this hurt begins to invade every other area of our life. We carry a heavy burden which we know we don't deserve - and which we certainly don't desire to keep - but it's a burden we can't seem to let go.

There is only one true way to relieve the burden of our hurt, and it always begins with forgiveness. True forgiveness can be difficult and require great humility. We want the other person to first ask (maybe even beg) for our forgiveness. We would like them to admit the hurt they caused; and, if we are honest, we probably would prefer them to suffer...just a little. But this is not in God's plan.

Colossians 3:13

> *"Bear with each other and forgive whatever grievances you may have against one another. Forgive as the Lord forgave you."*

If we have come to a saving faith in Jesus Christ, we have first come face to face with our sinful nature. Without an understanding that we are full of sin, we will never reach out for a savior. And if we have experienced the true meaning of God's love, "while we were still sinners, Christ died for us" (Romans 5:8), we will be compelled to forgive others. When we truly understand His forgiveness, we WILL forgive others!

Jesus told a parable of a man who failed to forgive a small debt when his master had just forgiven him a much greater debt: "'Shouldn't you have had mercy on your fellow servant just as I had on you?' In anger his master turned him over to the jailers to be tortured, until he should pay back all he owed" (Matthew 18:33-34). Do we really understand how much we have been forgiven? Or our inability to repay? Yet, our debt has been completely forgiven by grace through faith in Jesus and we are now commanded to forgive others.

God established the standard for forgiveness. We are not called to forgive because someone deserves or has earned our forgiveness, we are called to forgive simply because God first forgave us. When we forgive, we must strive to make the forgiveness complete; "For I will forgive their wickedness and will remember their sins no more" (Hebrews 8:12). Though we may carry a healthy level of new caution as the relationship continues, we must never place conditions on maintaining our forgiveness.

There WILL be times when we are burdened with hurt. But let's not seek revenge or try to withdraw and hide our pain. Let's follow the commands of God's Word and be set free! Let's grow closer to our Heavenly Father and see through His eyes. Let's share His love and forgive as He forgave.

WHAT IT MEANS TO FORGIVE

In the message "Forgive As He Forgave" we saw that our forgiveness of others should be based on recognizing the magnitude of forgiveness we've been given through faith in Jesus. A true understanding of God's mercy toward us compels us to be merciful to others. But still, forgiveness remains difficult and somewhat ambiguous. Some hurts last sooooo long!

There are those today trying to forgive child abusers, murderers, habitually unfaithful spouses, and a whole list of emotional and physical pain. How do we truly forgive when it hurts so much? And how do we know when we've properly forgiven?

Ephesians 4:31-32

> *"Get rid of all bitterness, rage and anger, brawling and slander, along with every form of malice. Be kind and compassionate to one another, forgiving each other, just as in Christ God forgave you."*

All forgiveness begins with a belief that God desires us to forgive in any situation; "If you do not forgive men their sins, your Father will not forgive your sins" (Matthew 6:15). If we are unable, or unwilling, to forgive, we need to spend more time reflecting on the forgiveness of Christ. Do we really understand? Do we really believe? Our ability to forgive identifies our focus: Is our priority on Christ or on our own needs and desires, hurts and pain?

But forgiveness is not simply saying the words "I forgive you." Rather, forgiveness is canceling the emotional debt. It means we love and earnestly pray for blessings in their life; "Love your enemies and pray for those who persecute you" (Matthew 5:44). We should be able to think about the other person without bitterness, rage, or anger. We should be able to pray for an increase in their ministry or business, more peace in their family, and a closer relationship with Jesus. It's amazing how much healing takes place in our own heart when we pray for those who have caused us pain.

However, forgiveness does not necessarily mean a relationship must continue as if the hurt never occurred. Our heart may be free of all anger and bitterness - we may earnestly pray for the one who caused us pain - and yet, we no longer trust or enjoy their company. My forgiveness of a child abuser does not require me to leave my children in their care. I can love with a Christ-like love and pray without anger and yet guard my physical body and emotional and Spiritual heart.

It's unfortunate, but most of us are carrying some bitterness toward another person today. These burdensome emotions should not continue in the heart of a Child of God, and the only road to release them is through the gate of forgiveness. Let's ask God to purify our heart. Let's refocus on the cross and release our burdens to Him. Let's honor our Father by showing the world what it means to forgive.

STEP OF FAITH

Today was a busy day! Early this morning we heard that King Herod killed John the Baptist. Jesus seemed to take this news pretty hard; "When Jesus heard what had happened, He withdrew by boat privately to a solitary place" (Matthew 14:13). I knew He wanted to be alone, but the crowds kept following Him. Soon there were "about five thousand men, besides women and children" (Matthew 14:21). When it started to get late we tried to send the people home, but Jesus had everyone sit down and He fed them with "five loaves of bread and two fish" (Matthew 14:17). What a day!!

Finally, Jesus sent us across the Sea of Galilee; "After leaving them, He went up on a mountain to pray" (Mark 6:46). I'm glad Jesus is getting some time alone, but I wish He was here right now. It's dark and the waves are so high. Wait, there's something out there; something, or someone, walking on the water; "It's a ghost, they said, and cried out in fear" (Matthew 6:26). No, I think it's Jesus!

Matthew 14:28-29

"'Lord, if it's You,' Peter replied, 'tell me to come to You on the water.' 'Come,' He said. Then Peter got down out of the boat, walked on the water and came toward Jesus."

When Peter took that first step onto the water, there was nothing within his physical senses which told him the water would hold. The boat was being tossed by the wind and waves, and Peter certainly had many past experiences telling him that heavy objects sink in water - telling him his step would fail.

But Peter KNEW Jesus. He had spent time with Jesus - he walked with Him, talked with Him, prayed with Him, and witnessed His miracles. Peter knew the face of Jesus and knew His voice. He knew if Jesus said "Come," He would also provide a way for him to follow. Jesus made the water solid, but only when and where Peter stepped - only after he stepped out in faith and in response to the call.

The step of faith is needed for any situation which requires a solution beyond what our physical senses can understand. "Now faith is being sure of what we hope for and certain of what we do not see" (Hebrews 11:1). The situation may be related to relationships, finances, jobs, or ministry opportunities. But it may also be related to raising children, challenges at school, the apparent inability to forgive, or anything else which requires us to operate outside the comfort of the boat.

God calls us to a life of faith. We must spend quality time with our Lord so we can recognize His voice, but when God says "Come," our only response is to step. Our past experiences may scream it's not possible and that we will fail. We may not see solid ground, but we must trust that the One who called will provide the solid foundation. Let's trust Him to provide a way with each and every step of faith!

FOCUSED ON JESUS

I've always been impulsive. I was one of the first to follow Jesus. I didn't even know who He was, and when He said "Come, follow Me, and I will make you fishers of men" (Matthew 4:19), I didn't even know what He meant, but I dropped my fishing nets and followed. After three years, I foolishly told Jesus I was "ready to go with You to prison and to death" (Luke 22:33), but that same night I denied I even knew Him - three times! And, in the garden, when the soldiers came to take Him away, I drew my sword "and struck the high priest's servant, cutting off his right ear" (John 18:10).

But the most impulsive thing I ever did was that night in the boat. The waves were rough and we had "rowed three or three and a half miles" (John 6:19), when I saw Jesus walking on the water. I told Him I would come if He called and the next thing I knew I was jumping out of the boat! And I didn't sink!! I kept my eyes on Jesus, I knew in my heart He was "the Christ, the Son of the living God" (Matthew 16:16), but the wind was blowing so hard and the waves kept crashing against my legs.

Matthew 14:30

"But when he {Peter} saw the wind, he was afraid and, beginning to sink, cried out, 'Lord, save me!'"

Jesus said Peter began to sink because he doubted and had little faith (Matthew 14:31), but let's not be too hard on Peter - remember, no one else even left the boat! Peter stepped out of the boat and took several steps on top of the water!! But then he lost his focus.

Peter was in the middle of an awesome display of God's power and yet he "saw the wind," or at least the effects of the wind. Peter began to look at the turbulence of the world and not at the One who created the world; "Let us fix our eyes on Jesus, the author and perfecter of our faith" (Hebrews 12:2).

There are times when we clearly see God's hand at work. Our eyes become focused on Jesus, His peace fills our life, and the foundation under our feet feels solid and secure. However, it's usually not long before the wind begins to blow, the waves rise up, and we feel that sinking feeling. When this happens (and it will) we must not despair, for this is also part of God's wonderful plan. As we are sinking, He always reaches out His hand as an invitation to draw near and know Him better - to know He will always be there when we cry out "Lord, save me!"

The walk of faith cannot be accomplished in our own strength. With each step we must "put to death whatever belongs to your earthly nature" (Colossians 3:5), and "clothe yourselves with the Lord Jesus Christ" (Romans 13:14). Every day we must take our eyes off our own ability and the pulls of the world - take our eyes off the wind - and commit to trusting and keeping our eyes focused on Jesus.

HEAR THE CALL

In the last two messages, we've considered Peter as he responded to Jesus' call: "Then Peter got down out of the boat, walked on the water and came toward Jesus" (Matthew 14:29). We saw that Peter needed great faith to step out of the boat, even though his faith quickly faded "when he saw the wind" (Matthew 14:30). But we also saw that before Peter could even get out of the boat, he first needed to hear and recognize the clear call of God; "Lord, if it is You, tell me to come to You on the water" (Matthew 14:28).

It wasn't faith alone which allowed Peter to walk on the water, he had to apply his faith to Jesus' call. It was Jesus who provided a firm foundation under Peter's feet as he stepped. Peter wasn't specially gifted at water walking - he simply heard the call and obeyed in faith.

If Peter would have sailed to the exact same spot the following day and stepped out of the boat without being called, he would have sunk like a heavy stone - guaranteed! Peter could not have commanded the water to hold nor "claimed" a solid foundation for His feet. His faith would not have kept him on top of the water for even a fraction of a second. His "success" on the water was not due as much to the magnitude of his faith as it was to properly hearing and then applying his faith to the call of Jesus.

John 10:27

"My sheep listen to My voice; I know them, and they follow Me."

We seem to spend much of our life wandering without direction, but it's God's desire that we follow closely after His Son; "He goes on ahead of them, and His sheep follow Him because they know His voice" (John 10:4). Do we really know His voice? How often do we set aside time to listen? If we only occasionally listen to the voice of our Lord, how will we even recognize His call? We live in a world so filled with distractions that we must not wait until the crisis of a storm. If we haven't learned to filter out the competing noises of the world, God's call will be lost in the crashing waves.

We must spend time away from the "noise" where we can be alone with God and learn to recognize His voice. We must establish times of quiet to read His Word and talk with Him in prayer; "Sanctify them by the truth; Your Word is truth" (John 17:17). As we meditate on the truth of His Word and pray for understanding, our Spiritual filter will become tuned. Then, when we enter a storm, the noise may still surround us, but our filter will only allow a single voice to enter.

Let's develop the discipline of listening along with the Spiritual ability to filter and recognize the voice of God. Our faith will be enough to respond - strong enough to step - but we must first be able to hear the call.

MEET THEM WHERE THEY ARE

Peter heard the call of Jesus in the middle of a storm and "got down out of the boat, walked on the water and came toward Jesus" (Matthew 14:29). Peter knew the voice of his Lord and knew that if He called, He would also provide a way to follow. But Peter soon "saw the wind...and, beginning to sink, cried out, 'Lord, save me!'" (Matthew 14:30).

Matthew 14:31-33

"Immediately Jesus reached out His hand and caught him. 'You of little faith,' He said, 'why did you doubt?' And when they climbed into the boat, the wind died down. Then those who were in the boat worshiped Him, saying, 'Truly You are the Son of God.'"

Jesus' words to Peter might seem a little harsh. After all, Peter had stepped onto the water while the other disciples remained in the boat. But Peter needed to be encouraged in what true faith could accomplish. He needed to clearly see that "with God all things are possible" (Matthew 19:26), but only if he kept his eyes focused on Jesus. God had great plans for Peter - plans which would require great faith - so Jesus ministered to Peter's doubts and fears by meeting him on the water.

Jesus then climbed in the boat with the other disciples. Rather than chastising them for their lack of faith and telling them how they should have climbed out of the boat, Jesus simply allowed them to worship. These disciples had failed to understand who He was, and now they needed to just spend time loving and worshiping their Lord. Jesus ministered to the needs of these disciples by meeting them in the boat.

The Apostle Paul had a clear understanding of ministry opportunities: "To the weak I became weak, to win the weak. I have become all things to all men so that by all possible means I might save some" (1 Corinthians 9:22). Paul never sinned in order to save the sinner, but he understood where a person was in their Spiritual journey and began his ministry right at that point.

Every day God places people in our life who need encouragement and desperately need to be directed onto a path which will lead them closer to God. None of us know all the answers, and we certainly don't need to force everything we know into a single conversation, but we each are given an opportunity to minister - an opportunity which may only last a moment and may never truly return.

Let's look for the specific needs of those who cross our path and be prepared to encourage with the truth of God's Word. But as we speak the truth, whether on the water, in the boat or even back on the shore, let's minister as we meet them where they are.

STEP TOWARD JESUS

In the last several messages, we consider the faith of Peter as he stepped out of the boat and walked on the water. We saw the importance of properly hearing the call and of keeping our eyes focused on our Lord as the waves are crashing at our feet. This story contains many lessons for our walk with Christ. But a lesson which is often overlooked is that of the motivation of the heart.

We know that the heart contains our true character and true relationship with our Heavenly Father. When God was showing Samuel who to anoint as king of Israel He reminded Him: "The Lord does not look at the things man looks at. Man looks at the outward appearance, but the Lord looks at the heart" (1 Samuel 16:7). Our outward actions are a "reflection" of the condition of our heart; but they are not a true image and they can most certainly deceive!

God saw this deception in the worship of His Children long ago. We are all susceptible to the trap of going through the motions of worship without really having a heart devoted to God: "These people come near to Me with their mouth and honor Me with their lips, but their hearts are far from Me. Their worship of Me is made up only of rules taught by men" (Isaiah 29:13).

Yes, without considering the heart we lose the real message of Peter getting out of the boat. These words become just another self-gratifying motivational speech for those who want to climb up another rung of the ladder: "If you want to go further and accomplish more, you must leave the security of the boat!" Taking a "step of faith" will often lead to "successful" advancement in worldly as well as ministry endeavors, but neither are pleasing to God without the proper heart.

We sometimes forget that there was another time when Peter got out of the boat, but this time Jesus was a little distance away standing on the shore.

John 21:7

"As soon as Simon Peter heard him say, "It is the Lord," he wrapped his outer garment around him (for he had taken it off) and jumped into the water."

Peter wasn't motivated by the thrill of walking on the water, not by the praise he might receive from the other disciples or even by the thought of doing something wonderful for God. Peter got out of the boat simply because that's where Jesus was; and, walk, sink or swim, he desired to be with the one he loved.

Let's pray for an increased faith which allows us to follow more closely after Jesus. Let's pray for the courage to leave the confines of our worldly security and follow where Jesus is calling. But let's diligently examine our heart and make sure that with EVERY step, we abandon all and step toward Jesus.

HOLD ME

In the message "Step Toward Jesus" we were encouraged to examine the motivation for the things we do and exhorted to do ALL things for the love of being closer to Jesus. This is the essence of our relationship with our Father - simple, but absolute love.

When a young child wants to be held, they simply reach up their arms and say: "Hold me!" Children may be hurt, scared, or tired; they may not even know why they want to be held, but they know that spending time in arms of love seems to make everything better.

And as a parent looks down at their child, they rarely evaluate them to determine if they deserve to be held, or send them away to earn affection; rather, they simply pick up the child and hold them with no words even being required. In truth, moments like this bring parents some of their greatest joy!

Matthew 18:3

"I tell you the truth, unless you change and become like little children, you will never enter the kingdom of heaven."

Our Heavenly Father loves us very much. He wants us to come to Him with outstretched arms. He wants to pick us up and hold us tight. In truth, moments like this bring His greatest joy! And yet, we spend most of our days avoiding our Father's loving arms. We seek other forms of comfort and work to earn our Father's affection. We pour our heart into projects thinking they are vitally important to God's work; "Daddy, look what I made for You!" But our best efforts are as grade school pencil holders and disfigured flower pots. Our Father smiles at these simple gifts but wishes we would understand.

There's much work to do for the Kingdom of God, but none more important than loving and being loved by the One who has loved us since the beginning of time; "Love the Lord your God with all your heart and with all your soul and with all your mind and with all your strength" (Mark 12:30).

This can be a difficult concept for many who have not grown up with the unconditional love and acceptance of an earthly father - but our Father in Heaven is like none we've ever known. He created us for a relationship of love and "gave His one and only Son" (John 3:16) so we could be restored to the relationship which sin stole away. Let there be no doubt of His love and His promise; "Never will I leave you; never will I forsake you" (Hebrews 13:5).

He longs for us to return! Yes, we must clean our room, take out the trash, and treat others nice on the playground - but at the end of the day, His greatest desire is that we reach up with empty arms and say: I love You Daddy - hold me!

REMAIN LIKE A CHILD

In the message "Hold Me" we saw how our Heavenly Father desires for us to reach up to Him with outstretched arms. We considered the example of a child reaching up to be held by their parent. This is where our relationship with God begins and, in many ways, it's where we must remain.

When the disciples asked Jesus, "Who is the greatest in the Kingdom of Heaven?" (Matthew 18:1), He responded with a harsh rebuke; "Unless you change and become like little children, you will never enter the Kingdom of Heaven" (Matthew 18:3). The disciples were arguing about their eternal "greatness" and Jesus said unless they changed they would not even enter Heaven! Obviously, following Jesus, listening to His teachings, and having a general belief is not enough.

Salvation, or as Jesus said, "enter{ing} the Kingdom of Heaven," involves a complete submission which understands our inability to save ourselves. We can do nothing but present the "filthy rags" (Isaiah 64:6) of our life and receive the mercy and forgiveness of a loving Father. Salvation is not something we rise up and achieve; rather, it's a gift for which we must submit and receive. When we understand this gift, we will be filled with such thankfulness that our only desire will be to love Him and do ALL to bring Him glory and honor.

Matthew 18:4

"Therefore, whoever humbles himself like this child is the greatest in the Kingdom of Heaven."

Becoming like a little child, dependent on Christ, is necessary for entering the Kingdom, but walking in humility as we grow is God's desire for our entire life. We are to be "conformed to the likeness of His Son" (Romans 8:29). But it was His Son "Who, being in very nature God, did not consider equality with God something to be grasped, but made Himself nothing...He humbled Himself and became obedient to death" (Philippians 2:6-8). We are being conformed to His humility.

The great temptation of Spiritual "growth" is to begin to think we have all the answers and desire to establish our own path with its own set of rules - we become like the know-it-all teenager. When this occurs, we must immediately, and with great determination, humble ourselves and put to death the rebellious pride which leads us astray. We must "trust in the Lord with all your heart and lean not on your own understanding" (Proverbs 3:5). We must daily remember the children we really are...and the children we need to continually become.

We must always continue to grow and mature. We must learn more of our Heavenly Father and His desire for our life, walk in faith and be obedient to all He has commanded. But we must also remember that as we grow, we are to walk in humility and remain like a child.

SACRIFICE OF WEAKNESS

In the message "Remain Like a Child" we considered our need to come to our Heavenly Father with an understanding that we have no ability to save ourself. We then saw our call to continually approach God like a little child approaching a loving Father; "whoever humbles himself like this little child is the greatest in the Kingdom of Heaven" (Matthew 18:4).

But, we say, surely God doesn't want us to remain as a child. Doesn't He want us to grow? Absolutely! Paul addressed the Corinthian Church as worldly rather than Spiritual because they were "mere infants in Christ" (1 Corinthians 3:1). The Church was experiencing many trials because they had failed to grow: "I gave you milk, not solid food, for you were not ready for it. Indeed, you are still not ready" (1 Corinthians 3:2).

God's Word never calls us to maintain the faith or Spiritual understanding of a child. These simple qualities are important, but we must continually grow and send down the deep roots which will weather the storm. What we are called to maintain is the simple humility of a child. We must learn to be secure in our Father's Hand and to "approach the throne of grace with confidence" (Hebrews 4:16), but we must never let our confidence and security lead to an ungrateful assumption of His grace. We initially came to God weak and helpless; and no matter how much we grow - no matter how deep our roots - we remain weak and unable to add a single grain to the grace which He has poured over us.

But our weakness is good! In fact, an understanding of our weakness apart from Christ and our continued walk of weakness is one of the few offerings we can give to our Lord.

2 Corinthians 12:9,10

> *"'My grace is sufficient for you, for My power is made perfect in weakness.' ...That is why, for Christ's sake, I delight in weaknesses, in insults, in hardships, in persecutions, in difficulties. For when I am weak, then I am strong."*

God has chosen to unfold His plan through the lives of His children. We are to reflect the light of Christ into a dark and lifeless world; "We are therefore Christ's ambassadors, as though God were making His appeal through us" (2 Corinthians 5:20). And the world will best see Christ as we remove our own perceived strength and allow the power of God to freely work through us: His power is made perfect as I get my "self" out of the way and walk with a humble weakness.

It's interesting that one of the greatest things we can give to God is an understanding of what we do not have. Let's strip away our pride and once again approach Him with empty hands. Let's offer our lives as a living sacrifice, as a humble sacrifice of weakness.

JARS OF CLAY

In the message "Sacrifice of Weakness" we saw how one of our greatest gifts we can give our Heavenly Father is the recognition of how little we have to give. It's a wonderful mystery that the Almighty God can reach so far down and lift us up, through the gift of His Son and the power of the Holy Spirit, and elevate us to the position of "co-heirs with Christ" (Romans 8:17).

Through faith in Jesus, we experience a new birth and are given the gift of eternal life. This is an incredible gift, almost more than we can imagine! Through faith in Jesus, the Creator of the Universe transforms our heart; "I will remove from you your heart of stone and give you a heart of flesh" (Ezekiel 36:26), and He makes His dwelling within us. This message of Salvation can change lives...and we have been called to take this message to the world!!

2 Corinthians 4:7

"But we have this treasure in jars of clay to show that this all-surpassing power is from God and not from us."

God has chosen to entrust this message of forgiveness, this "ministry of reconciliation" (2 Corinthians 5:18), this most valuable treasure, to us - common jars of clay! In Paul's day these jars were very ordinary vessels, easily chipped or broken, and often flawed. How beautifully appropriate!

Our flaws actually serve a purpose in God's plan, for our jars of clay show that the message which shines in and through our life is from God and not from us. When we truly place our faith and trust in Jesus, we are forever changed: we become "a new creation; the old has gone, the new has come!" (2 Corinthians 5:17). The new has come, and the new is different - but "the new" is definitely not perfect!!

Paul himself was far from perfect: "Who is weak, and I do not feel weak? Who is led into sin, and I do not inwardly burn?" (2 Corinthians 11:29). But Paul had been clearly taught by Jesus that his weakness served the purpose of bringing the ultimate glory and honor to God: "My grace is sufficient for you, for My power is made perfect in weakness" (2 Corinthians 12:9).

This doesn't mean we should make light of sin or give less than our very best, but we must begin to view our weaknesses as opportunities to depend more on God and to keep our focus more on Christ. As we trust Him more, His power will be made perfect in us.

This also means that the flaws which inevitably surface in those around us are also part of God's plan. These flaws afford us the opportunity to demonstrate grace, forgiveness, and love. One day when we are taken to be with Jesus we will be made perfect; but for now, we're ALL jars of clay.

PASS THE BLESSING

When Jesus began His ministry on earth, He taught those who had an ear to hear, healed those who were sick, and fed those who were hungry. He also selected twelve Apostles and sent them "to the lost sheep of Israel" (Matthew 10:6) with instructions to preach, heal, and feed. As He was preparing them for the mission field, He gave a command to maintain a giving heart.

Matthew 10:8

"Freely you have received, freely give."

All we have is from the hand of God. There is nothing we can claim we have earned or deserve. If the material in this book has in any way blessed you and helped to draw you closer to God, I pray you would consider giving this book to someone else. Our Heavenly Father will continue to be glorified as we freely pass the blessing!

I included this message at the end of this book (as well as at the end of "Volume 1") as a way of encouraging people to share these books with others. These messages have only limited value if they are read once and put on the shelf.

But there is a much more general principle at work, and one much more important than the

121

sharing of books. We have received from God the greatest gift of all, the gift of His Son. God gave His Son, free of charge to all who believe, as a full and complete sacrifice for the forgiveness of our sin. We may take the rest of our lives trying to comprehend the magnitude of this gift, but He has given us a way to spend all eternity with Him in Heaven. He has given us a ticket which instantly transports us from eternal death in Hell to eternal life in Heaven. Can anything compare? Yet the gift is free.

The gift is free and absolutely not for sale. We cannot purchase eternal life with all the money in the world or all the good deeds accomplished by every soul who ever walked the earth. The only way to receive the gift of eternal life is to humbly approach the Giver and believe.

But now that we have received such a wonderful gift we must give it away. We cannot keep the gift of Salvation on the shelf and hope to dust it off when we're finally called Home. We must share our faith - share our gift - with anyone, anywhere, and at any time that will be able to express His love and glorify His name. Our ability to give away the gift reflects an understanding of its value and the free grace through which it was given. Let's share the free gift of Jesus with others today. Today, let's freely pass the blessing.